The Gospels' Veiled Agenda

Revolution, Priesthood and
The Holy Grail

First published by O Books, 2009
O Books is an imprint of John Hunt Publishing Ltd., The Bothy, Deershot Lodge, Park Lane, Ropley,
Hants, SO24 0BE, UK
office1@o-books.net
www.o-books.net

Distribution in:	South Africa
	Stephan Phillips (pty) Ltd
UK and Europe	Email: orders@stephanphillips.com
Orca Book Services	Tel: 27 21 4489839 Telefax: 27 21 4479879
orders@orcabookservices.co.uk	
Tel: 01202 665432 Fax: 01202 666219	Text copyright Harry Freedman 2008
Int. code (44)	
	Design: Stuart Davies
USA and Canada	
NBN	ISBN: 978 1 84694 260 0
custserv@nbnbooks.com	
Tel: 1 800 462 6420 Fax: 1 800 338 4550	All rights reserved. Except for brief quotations
	in critical articles or reviews, no part of this
Australia and New Zealand	book may be reproduced in any manner without
Brumby Books	prior written permission from the publishers.
sales@brumbybooks.com.au	
Tel: 61 3 9761 5535 Fax: 61 3 9761 7095	The rights of Harry Freedman as author have
	been asserted in accordance with the
Far East (offices in Singapore, Thailand,	Copyright, Designs and Patents Act 1988.
Hong Kong, Taiwan)	
Pansing Distribution Pte Ltd	
kemal@pansing.com	A CIP catalogue record for this book is available
Tel: 65 6319 9939 Fax: 65 6462 5761	from the British Library.

Printed by Digital Book Print

O Books operates a distinctive and ethical publishing philosophy in
all areas of its business, from its global network of authors to
production and worldwide distribution.

The Gospels' Veiled Agenda

Revolution, Priesthood and
The Holy Grail

Harry Freedman

BOOKS

Winchester, UK
Washington, USA

CONTENTS

For Josh and Mollie. Their inspiration and creativity.
And special thanks to Karen.

1

The Failed Revolution

The revolution failed before it even got started. Yet its consequences had an impact way beyond the rebels' wildest dreams. The revolution was supposed to overthrow the complacent leaders of a small, globally irrelevant religion. It didn't even manage to do that. But its aftermath changed the world.

And the funny thing is, that although the revolution failed and was scrubbed out of history, we can still find out all about it in the world's best known book. If we only understand what we are reading.

But because the world's best known book is the Bible, and because we are taught to approach the bible seeking religious truth and inspiration, we rarely consider that it is also a chronicle of its times, containing snippets of factual information that don't necessarily enhance the spiritual message, but that tell us a lot about the real world in which its heroes lived.

The revolution failed because the men who were its target called in the foreign power who ruled over the territory. They, wary of unrest amongst their subject population, savagely executed the two most prominent figures. We know the story but we don't appreciate the context.

We find the story of the rebellion in the four gospels, written by the Evangelists: Matthew, Mark, Luke and John. The rebellion is just one piece of historical information that they contain; information that the church has not always wished to see made public.

These four books constitute the core of the New Testament. They are the fundamental texts of Christianity, the classic histories of Jesus's life. Three of these, Matthew, Mark, and Luke are known collectively as the synoptic gospels, because they provide a similar view of the life and teachings of Jesus[1]. The fourth, the gospel of John is markedly different, as we shall see. There is so much uncertainty surrounding the gospel of John that even its name is in doubt; many scholars prefer to refer to it simply as the Fourth Gospel.

Nobody would deny the inspirational power of the gospels. But however powerful they are as religious texts, they are more than this. They also are historical documents; four separate accounts by four separate authors of the life and times of Jesus of Nazareth. Apart from being the basis of all Christian belief, they are the earliest records that exist of the life of Jesus. Woven into their religious teachings is valuable information about many aspects of day to day life in the province of Judea, the Roman occupiers' name for Israel, during the first half of the first century. That in itself is not controversial. But what may be disturbing to some is the significant, although not necessarily obvious, information about the true hopes and ambitions of Jesus and his followers. Aspirations that did not necessarily fit with Christianity as we have come to know it.

The gospels tell us about the revolution that failed, the quashed rebellion that changed the world. And in so doing they tell us much more as well; they speak of matters which were not necessarily welcomed by the architects of Christianity, subjects which, in their eyes, were better not spoken of. Subjects which, because of their controversial nature, appear in the gospels in coded form only. They may once have been more explicit but later editors concealed them. They leave the reader to work out what the Evangelists – as the gospel authors are known- were really trying to tell us. We can only fully understand this if we put the religious doctrines of Christianity on one side and approach the gospels with a critical and incisive eye.

Of course that is not so easy to do. We have been conditioned to read the gospels in a certain way, in the way that the founders of the Christian religion wanted them to be read. It is no secret that the architect of Christianity, Paul of Tarsus, radically shaped the popular image of Jesus of Nazareth. Paul, who lived at the same time as the authors of the gospels, had never met Jesus. For much of his life he was a bitter enemy of the emerging Christian religion. But he was converted, on the road to Damascus, and he spent the rest of his life travelling widely and spreading the new Christian message to non believers. He wrote many letters to communities across the Mediterranean and Middle East. Some of these letters, which were really small pamphlets, were lost. Some appear in the New Testament. Letters to the Romans, Corinthians, Thessalonians and Hebrews, amongst others. Paul emphasised the spiritual and religious aspects of Jesus's life and teachings which he believed, correctly, would appeal to the masses. He played down those aspects which he felt did not support the theology he wanted to promote, including much of the historical evidence. The image of Jesus as portrayed by Paul became the familiar one, and when we read the Evangelists' gospels we read them refracted through Paul's lens. We pay attention to the bits that present Jesus religiously, we don't really think about the bits which seem to have little spiritual connection. We see Jesus as Paul wanted us to see him. We do not see the other Jesus, Jesus the man, Jesus the Jew, Jesus the politician.

The philosopher Friedrich Nietzsche, who was particularly scathing about Paul, claimed in his work The Antichrist[2] that 'God as Paul created him, is the negation of God'. Paul, as we shall see, even wrote the Holy Grail out of Christianity, believing that it was too dangerous to retain.

Paul's great talent was to draw out of Jesus's life those events and teachings that would inspire the world. But in so doing he had to play down events recorded in the gospels that were concerned with Jesus's personal agenda. It wasn't that Paul disapproved of, or wanted to disguise, Jesus's human ambitions. But to focus attention on them when he was trying to teach a much more profound religious message would have muddied the waters. Every good marketeer knows- and Paul was probably the best marketeer ever- that you don't give your audience mixed messages. So the gospels contain all sorts of incongruous information that just doesn't fit with Pauline Christianity, that appears to be parenthetical and which can only be fully understood when read from a historical perspective, rather than a religious one.

The Evangelists and Paul all lived and worked at the same time. It is quite easy to date them because they are all aware of Jesus's crucifixion which took place round about the year 37, and none of them seem to be aware of the destruction of Jerusalem between the years 66-70. Jerusalem sits at the heart of the Jesus story- it is where he spent much of his life and where he died. The city and the temple were so important to them and the destruction of Jerusalem was an event of such magnitude for the Jewish nation to which Paul and the Evangelists belonged, that it is inconceivable that they would have not mentioned it in their writings if it had already taken place.

So the gospels and Paul's letters are all composed within a window of time that was less than 30 years. They all dealt with the same subject and there is little doubt that they influenced each other. Most scholars agree that Matthew and Luke's gospels were based on Mark's. The gospels, in the form that we have them, were written in Greek whilst their Jewish authors spoke Aramaic. So it is quite likely that these books, which were probably oral Aramaic compositions, went through a process of revision and editing by Greek speaking editors before they reached their final forms. And it is possible that part of the editing process included bringing some of the content of the gospels into line with Paul's thinking, since his approach was emerging as the dominant form of Christianity. It is even possible that the original gospels that the Evangelists wrote, or dictated, may have been edited so much that very little remains of their final form. But the versions we have today still include enough of the controversial, factual information for us to appreciate that they contain more than meets the eye.

First century Jewish and Christian texts are very different from modern literature. Just as there is a way of appreciating Homer or Chaucer, so too is there a way of reading the genre that includes the gospels. So, to identify the factual information that interests us, and appreciate what the Evangelists were really trying to say we will have to understand more about the way they wrote as well as the issues that mattered to them. Issues which, as it turned out were not only irrelevant to Christianity as it finally emerged, but which actually threatened it.

It may appear obvious but we should be aware that the Evangelists did not set out to write a Bible. In fact they had never heard of such a thing. For although the books of the Jewish Bible, the Old Testament[3] would have been well known to them, and these books were the revealed texts of the Jews, nobody considered them to be a Bible. No religious authority had yet declared them sacred[4]. The concept of Bible was yet to be invented and there is no reason to believe that the Evangelists, or Paul for that matter had the intention of writing a 'Holy Book'. The gospels are chronicles of Jesus's life, and were probably never intended as anything else. Indeed the word Bible, deriving from the Greek word for a book is probably a late Christian invention. It was the Christian church, many centuries later which formally declared them the opening books of a canonical text, at a synod in Rome in 382 CE.[5]

If the Evangelists weren't trying to write a bible but they were telling the story of Jesus, then to what purpose? When a biographer writes about a famous character they do so because they believe there will be an audience out there who finds the subject compelling or at least interesting. But clearly the gospel authors wanted their readers to do more than find Jesus interesting. They would have wanted their audience to revere and believe in Jesus. They were anxious that his teachings and his message would be heard. And they wanted the truth about his life to be known. All of which indicates that the gospels were intended to inspire, to educate and most of all to promote knowledge of Jesus as a spiritual and religious leader. Possibly even to declare him as Messiah, although there is some doubt as to whether the gospels actually do this, or just hint at the possibility.

Fighting in the Temple

But the mix of inspirational portrayal and historical fact leads to apparent contradictions. If the gospels are trying to promote Jesus as an inspirational, possibly messianic figure, then why do they tell us of the puzzling episode which occurs when Jesus is arrested? An episode which seems to contradict everything that Jesus and his disciples stood for. Although they seem to relate it almost in passing, we read that a fight took place, during which the apostle Peter cuts off the right ear of the high priest's servant, The passage stands out like a sore thumb. Fighting and violence seem to be the very antithesis of everything that the apostles believed, but there it is, in black and white, in every one of the four gospels[6]. And although Jesus protests against the violence, the story passes without any explanation. Is there more here than is apparent at first sight?

Then there is the occasion when Judas complains that one of Jesus's followers has poured an expensive perfume onto his feet. Judas argues that the perfume was worth a year's wages and wonders why Jesus didn't stop her. Jesus's reply doesn't fit with the image of a man who has no interest in material goods, which is how we perceive him today. "Leave her alone," Jesus replied. "It was intended that she should save this perfume for the day of my burial. You will always have the poor among you but you will not always have me."[7]

6

Or the famous incident when Jesus throws the money-changers out of the Temple. Contrary to church dogma, Jesus is unlikely to have been offended by their presence in the sacred court, in fact he does not even criticise them for being there:

Then Jesus went into the Temple and drove out those who bought and sold in the Temple, and overturned the tables of the money changers and the seats of those who sold doves. And he said to them, 'It is written, 'My house shall be called a house of prayer,[8] *but you have made it a den of thieves.'*[9]

The implication, in church teachings, is that Jesus is purifying the Temple for prayer and divine service by ridding it of traders and traffickers whose base materialism had corrupted the holy place.

In fact the money changers and bird sellers were there legitimately. They were an essential part of the hustle and bustle of daily Temple life. There were various events in the life of every Israelite when they were obliged, or chose, to bring a sacrifice. These included recovery from sickness, thanksgiving for childbirth, the failure to perform a religious duty, the fulfilment of a vow or simply as a voluntary gesture. In addition people brought sacrifices at each festival, offered up the firstborn of their cattle and sheep, and in most years were expected to bring a tenth of their produce to Jerusalem for a festive meal.

Generally people did not bring animals or food all the way from their homes to Jerusalem, but travelled with their money and purchased the sacrifices on the spot. This explains what the dove sellers were doing in the Temple. A dove was the sacrifice brought by a poor person who could afford nothing else; in the days of the Roman occupation the vast majority of people were poor.[10]

The money changers had a similar right to be there. They enabled people to bring the annual poll tax. Everybody was obliged to bring a silver half-shekel for the upkeep of the sanctuary; this was a ceremonial coin that was not necessarily in common currency. People would go to the money changer's table to exchange their everyday coins, which, unlike today's money were valued by weight, for ceremonial shekels. The second century Mishnah, effectively the Jewish legal constitution, derives case law from these principles:

> *In Jerusalem, money may be changed again, silver coins for other silver coins, copper coins for other copper coins, silver for copper, and copper back into fruit.*[11]
>
> *Money found in the Temple is deemed to be common currency but if found (anywhere) in Jerusalem during the festival season it is deemed to be tithes.*[12]

We can only speculate at what the traders were doing which offended Jesus. There probably was cheating going on, the phrase 'den of thieves' certainly suggests so. But the point is not that Jesus was offended by the presence of traders in the Temple, it was their specific actions which disturbed him.

All these events, and many others, such as the soldiers gambling at the crucifixion, and Jesus's mystical transfiguration upon a mountain top contain evidence that there was a much more political side to Jesus than the image which Paul promoted. And as we begin to appreciate what Jesus was really trying to do we will coincidentally resolve other questions that remain troublesome when the gospels are read exclusively as religious literature. Questions that include Jesus's view on whether he was the Messiah, the true identity of Barabbas and, astonishingly, discovering what the Holy Grail actually was and what it signified.

So, what was Jesus's real agenda, and what are the gospels really trying to tell us?

The Roman Occupation

Jesus, his disciples and the people they lived amongst were all Jews. They spoke Aramaic, a Semitic language not dissimilar to Hebrew. They had a proud history, their own, long established religion, and a tribal identity which distinguished them from the other nations and clans who lived in the first century Middle Eastern melting pot. But their land had been conquered by Rome, and the Roman empire ruled the region with a terrible hand.

By all accounts the Roman occupation of Israel was one of the most brutal military occupations in history. Over the course of two centuries the Romans decimated the Jewish population, prohibited the practice of their religion, destroyed their Temple and enslaved them by the thousands. The Jews were a religious people, and they believed that whatever happened to them happened for a reason. In their minds they must have displeased God and the suffering that they were going through was evidently a punishment. Jewish texts of the first and second centuries are replete with theological debate seeking to understand the reasons for their suffering. The concept that suffering purifies, widely assumed to be a Christian innovation based on the Passion of Jesus, also finds expression in Jewish sources of the period. An early Jewish source explains the biblical verse: "Those who love me and keep my commandments" (Exodus 20,6) as:

These are the Jews who live in the land of Israel who risk their lives for the commandments. 'Why are you being taken out to be executed?' 'Because I circumcised my son.' 'Why are you being taken out to be burnt?' 'Because I read from the Torah.' 'Why are you being taken out to be crucified?' 'Because I ate the Passover bread.' 'Why are you being flogged?' 'Because I took the ritual palm branch.'

Other Jewish sources of the same period try to provide comfort by explaining the suffering theologically:

Rabbi Yose ben Rabbi Yehuda said 'Beloved is suffering for God's name alights upon those who suffer for him.[13]
When Rabbi Eliezer fell sick four of his colleagues came to visit him came to visit him. (Each in turn lamented his impending departure from the world. The fourth), Rabbi Akiva, said 'suffering is beloved'. Rabbi Eliezer (who had silently endured the tributes of the other three) said to them 'Sit me up so that I can hear the words of my pupil Akiva, who says that suffering is beloved.'[14]

However comforting it may, or may not, have been for ordinary people to have their suffering justified in theological terms, in practice the Jews were desperate for someone, anyone, who would come along and save them. The historian Josephus, a Jewish military commander who defected to the Romans and became a citizen of that nation, names several individuals who briefly flourished as leaders and promised to restore national sovereignty to the people. These included the so-called Zealots, Judah the Galilean and his companion Zadok who urged people to stop paying tribute to Rome and to return to God.[15] A certain Theudas encouraged people to take up their possessions and follow him to the Jordan river.[16] Others who bore the promise of redemption included Menahem ben Judah and Simeon bar Giora, both leaders of a briefly successful revolt against Rome in 66 CE. There was no shortage of would be saviours. If, as some claim today, Jesus was plotting a rebellion against Rome one might expect that Josephus would include him in his accounts of would be saviours. But Josephus, who is well aware of who Jesus was, does not include him in this context. And the gospels do not suggest that Jesus had military ambitions. Jesus's political strat-agems were not directed against the Romans.

Apart from the physical trauma of occupation, the isolated

Jewish community in the Holy Land was also under siege culturally. It was falling under the growing influence of Jewish Hellenists, cosmopolitans mainly from the Greek-Egyptian city of Alexandria, whose lifestyles were far more dissolute, and whose philosophy far more hedonistic than anything the nation had known for centuries. This internal clash of Jewish cultures, together with the loss of Israel's political independence, the personal suffering and ongoing armed struggles against the occupiers, precipitated a profound insecurity within the Jewish world. The land was in turmoil, politically, militarily, spiritually and emotionally. Judaism itself fragmented into different camps of which Pharisee, Sadducee, and Essene were just the best known. Meanwhile, other religions, Gnostics, Zoroastrian dualists, and Hellenist mystics all began to make their pitch to a lost generation, desperate for answers and for comfort.[17]

Wandering Charismatics

Into a world of despair and suffering, a new class of free-thinking and religious minded leaders emerged; men who could make sense of the suffering, and who would hold out a lamp in the darkness to those who followed behind. These men were itinerant preachers and miracle workers, independent souls who held no truck with the religious or political establishment of the day and who attracted a large personal following and a popular reputation. They gave hope to the despondent nation. They offered the promise of salvation. There were quite a few of them.

One was John the Baptist. John was a cousin, teacher, and erstwhile colleague of Jesus.

In those days John the Baptist came, preaching in the wilderness of Judea and saying, 'Repent, because the kingdom of heaven has come near!' For he is the one spoken of through the prophet Isaiah, who said: A voice of one crying out in the wilderness: 'Prepare the way for the lord; make his paths straight!' John himself had a camel-hair garment with a leather belt around his waist, and his food was locusts and wild honey. Then Jerusalem, all Judea, and all the vicinity of the Jordan were flocking to him, and they were baptized by him in the Jordan River as they confessed their sins.[18]

Jewish sources also recount the exploits of other first-century, miracle working preachers with popular followings. Men such as Honi HaMa'agel said to be a direct descendant of Moses[19] whose name means 'the drawer of circles'.

It once happened that people said to Honi Ha-Ma'agel: 'Pray for rain'. He said to them, bring your ovens indoors so that they do not spoil. He prayed but no rain came. He drew a circle, stood inside it and said 'Lord of the Universe, your children have turned to me, because I am like one of your own household. I swear by your name that I will not move from here until you have mercy upon your children.' Droplets of rain began to fall. He said: 'I did not ask you for this, but for rain that will fill pits, cisterns and caves. It began to rain in torrents. He said: 'I did not ask you for this, but for rain of favour and blessing, freely given.' It began to fall as he had ordained, until the people left the City of Jerusalem for the Temple, to shelter from the rain. They came and said to him: Just as you prayed for it to rain, now we beg you, pray for it to stop... .Shimon ben Shetach[20] said to him: If you were not Honi, I would excommunicate you. But what can I do, seeing that you sin before God, and he does as you ask, like a child who disobeys his father and still gets his own way[21]

Then there was Hanina ben Dosa. He was summoned by the inhabitants of a certain village where an Arod, a species of poisonous snake, had been killing local inhabitants. When he arrived in the village the snake had retreated to its hole in the ground. Hanina marched over and placed his bare foot over the snake's hole. The snake of course bit him. But Hanina was unharmed and the snake died. 'Woe to the person who meets an Arod. But woe to the Arod that meets Hanina ben Dosa.'[22]

Hanina ben Dosa heals the sick,[23] controls the rain through his prayers,[24] and in short does everything a miracle worker is supposed to do. But although he performs miracles, this is not what he is best remembered for. After all, every ancient culture had miracle men, most of whom are soon forgotten. Hanina's miracles may be evidence of his quirkiness but on their own they are not enough to establish his reputation. What set him apart was his wisdom and learning. His aphorisms are still quoted today:

> *Rabbi Hanina ben Dosa said, 'When one puts fear of wrongdoing ahead of wisdom, his wisdom will endure, but when he puts wisdom ahead of fear of wrongdoing, his wisdom will not endure. He would say, Anyone whose good deeds exceed his wisdom, his wisdom will endure. When his wisdom exceeds his good deeds, his wisdom will not endure.'*[25]

Honi also had a reputation as a scholar. He is said to have slept for seventy years. Upon waking he meets his grandson who, assuming him to be long dead, does not believe who he is. So Honi goes to the study house where he hears the scholars exclaiming that a certain matter of law had just been explained to them as clearly as if they had lived in the days of Honi Ha-Ma'agel, who when he went to the study house, would clarify all difficulties.[26]

And Jesus who of course performed miracles and wonders also had a reputation as a scholar. On one occasion he became involved in a confrontation in which he displayed a detailed knowledge of Jewish law, and highlighted apparent inconsistencies in the regulations which prohibit healing on the Sabbath. It came about because he had been criticised for curing a paralysed man on the Sabbath. Jesus argued that since circumcision, which affects only one part of the body can be carried out on Sabbath, it is surely logical that the whole body can be treated on that day.

Moses gave you circumcision ... and you circumcise a man on the Sabbath. If a man receives circumcision on the Sabbath ... are you angry with me because I made a man completely well on the Sabbath?[27]

Jesus, John the Baptist, Honi, Hanina ben Dosa, and several other, lesser known characters in ancient Jewish literature each possessed an ability to perform supernatural acts. Their power was directly connected to their wisdom and learning. In fact the need to be learned is such an important element in miracle working that even sages whose primary reputation rests in their scholarship, rather than their wonder working, do on occasion perform miracles because of their scholarly prowess. Rava, a leading rabbinic authority in fourth-century Babylon creates a golem, a living humanoid made from clay.[28] The legal authorities Shimon bar Yohai and his son Elazar, who spend twelve years in a cave hiding from the Roman authorities, become so intense of spirit that their gaze sets fire to whatever they direct it upon. They are sent back to the cave for a further year, to calm down, after which they emerge with more manageable powers.[29]

Although we have far more information about Jesus than any of the other esoteric sages it is clear that he fits the mould. Like them, he is not just a miracle worker, he is a scholar[30] and sage. He even teaches in the Temple, the very heart of the Jewish religion.[31]

Jesus was a hero for his times; he was exactly what people wanted. But because he was by no means the only itinerant charismatic to live in Roman Palestine, those who believed in him and wanted the world to know what he really stood for, would have an uphill struggle getting their message across, unless they could find a particularly effective way of presenting their story. To promulgate Jesus and to stress both his message and his personal, political agenda, the gospels themselves would need to be more inspirational than anything that had ever gone before. They would need to be couched in terms that struck a chord with the people the authors wanted to reach. They needed to speak directly to their audience and their audience needed to recognise them for what they were. And so, for us to understand how to read the gospels in order to extract and distil their historical information, we need to appreciate how the Evangelists went about their literary task, to recognise the literary techniques and cultural conventions that went into their composition.

When Hillary Clinton ran for the nomination to be the US Democratic candidate for President, her website emphasised the fact that she was a mother, that she "knows her scriptures", that she had been one of America's foremost advocates for children and families. The message that her supporters put out about her was designed to chime with those elements in the American population whom they most wanted to influence. In contrast, Rudy Giuliani, one of the Republican candidates, emphasised his promise to keep the American dream alive; and his record as a crime fighter. His campaign team targeted a different audience, and their message was framed in different terms.

Of course American presidential hopefuls have sophisticated marketing teams who work very hard to present their leaders in the most effective way. But the same phenomenon, of creating images by using terms that depend upon specific cultural awareness has always existed in literature. Fashionable patois, references to Hollywood figures, allusions to hip-hop or rock 'n roll only have meaning to people who are familiar with certain aspects of contemporary Western culture. And when an author uses these phrases they do so expecting that their readers will, through a process of cultural resonance, become more engaged with what they are reading.

Similarly, when we take a piece of literature and investigate the cultural influences, inspiration, and sources that it contains we begin to see it in a different light. The Merchant of Venice, for example, is based upon two romantic tales using themes that were widely recognised in the sixteenth century. One tale, attributed to a certain Ser Giovanni of Florence, appears in Il Pecorone, an Italian collection of short stories. This story provides Shakespeare with the main outline of the plot of his play, as well as its principle characters. The pound of flesh motif on the other hand could have come from several sources, the most likely being Alexander Silvayn's The Orator. The literary style of the play meanwhile, is a development of Shakespeare's earlier comedies.

But the fact that The Merchant of Venice uses themes that were familiar to its audience, and can be deconstructed into a combination of earlier tales, takes nothing away from the majesty, grandeur, and sheer genius of the play. Indeed it enhances the work; a familiar story is recast in an even more striking format. At the same time, as they spot its sources and hear familiar material presented in a new way, an audience's interest rises. They engage more fully. And a modern reader, who is able to deconstruct the literature into its component sources and influences, learns far more about Shakespeare, about the people he wrote for, and about the times that they lived in, than a mere reading of the play itself ever could teach her.

We can apply the same reasoning to the way the gospels were composed. Their early popularity was because they contained themes which were already familiar and culturally reassuring to the readers for whom they were written. Almost certainly the audience for whom the gospel writers wrote were not as surprised as we might have imagined to read about events such as virgin birth, or resurrection. They may have come across things like this before; such ideas may have been part of their cultural make-up. Encountering familiar motifs may have enabled them to relate to Jesus much more easily. In much the same way that an apprehensive audience at the premiere of a

Shakespeare play would have settled into it much more easily once they were reassured that they would see a powerful household lain low, a murder or two and quite likely a pure love turned to tragedy.

The gospel writers were Jews, and since they could write, it is reasonable to assume that they were educated men who were familiar with their own cultural heritage. They lived in a world of few books and no other media and the literature they did have was therefore hugely influential. Their bible, the Old Testament although they did not know it as such, was their literary, cultural, and religious framework. It contained their laws, history, poetry, and beliefs. It defined the way they thought, and influenced the way their society was structured. Even simple, uneducated peasants were familiar with its stories and the lives of its heroes, whilst the educated classes used it as virtually the sole authority for their legislation, economic structure, system of justice, and of course their religion.

Which is why the writers of the gospels chose to reflect the style and content of their existing, Jewish bible in their new works. To use the so-called Old Testament as a template and source book for the New. To cast their writings in the footprint of what had gone before and to incorporate echoes of the past in the new future they were creating. And so, for us to understand the New, to find out what the gospels are really telling us, and why, we need look further at its dependence upon the Old.

2

A Patriarchal Archetype

Although the Evangelists had no concept of Bible, they did know what a sacred text was. The Jewish religion was founded upon holy books, chief amongst which were the Five Books of Moses, known to the Jews as Torah and to the Greeks as Pentateuch. Other books, in the as yet informal Jewish canon, included Psalms, Kings, Proverbs and Job. There were also many other books which were not considered to be holy but which were known to educated Jews; these included Jubilees[32] and the Books of the Maccabees[33].

No-one knows for sure who wrote most of these books, their origins are lost in the mists of time. The faithful believe that they are the word of God, the rationalists that they are the product of human insight.[34] All agree that collectively these books constitute one of the great literary endeavours of the human race. Their epics, teachings, and morality thunder down through the ages. A multitude of heroes swarm through their pages, they were composed from two languages, Hebrew and Aramaic, with traces of half a dozen others, their style and literary structure can vary from page to page. These books have spawned dozens of cultures, spoken to hundreds of generations, suffered thousands of interpretations, and have been subjected to prodigious citations and myriads of criticisms.

The Evangelists knew that if they could produce literature which could stand alongside the existing tomes, in majesty, style and content they would stand a much better chance of engagement with their readers. But whereas the Jewish literature contains epics and legends that extend over many centuries, and which feature countless heroes, the story the Evangelists wanted to tell was rooted in one brief moment in time. It started with the birth of Jesus, and ended shortly after his death. All the characters in all the gospels would play supporting roles to Jesus, the one hero of the genre but one whom the Evangelists believed to be more important than all the celebrities of, what came to be termed, the Old Testament put together. The material that they would select for inclusion, the associations to be formed in the in the minds of the gospel readers, the image that was to be painted of Jesus himself; all this would be critical in determining whether the message that the Evangelists sought to bring to the world, Jesus's message, would endure for centuries, or whether it would just be another blip in the already long history of the Jews.

And what better chance did they have of giving their works immortality than to cast them in the mould of the earlier Jewish literature? To portray Jesus as the latest in a long line of Jewish religious leaders, a man whose spiritual and leadership characteristics were drawn from well established and deeply respected sources. To project fundamental Jewish mythic narratives into the Jesus epic. To inform their Jewish world of Jesus's teachings and political goals, and to stir up popular support.

This technique was wholly consistent with the way that much of the earlier literature had been constructed; either as a result of external influences from other cultures or otherwise using internal correspondences, ideas for one book drawn from another.

Complex works, such as the Hebrew bible can contain internal influences. One such is example occurs in the Book of Esther, a relatively late work in the Jewish Bible. Like many such books it recounts events that took place long before it was composed. It admits as much in its opening sentence:

'It once happened in the days of Ahasuerus,[35] that is the Ahasuerus who reigned from India to Ethiopia, one hundred and twenty seven *provinces.'*[36]

The Book of Esther is a tale of court intrigue, ostentatious wealth, callous rulers, defenceless victims, and brave heroes. A great story but why a sacred book? It does not contain any reference to God and its action takes place in Persia, making it the only canonical text set outside either Israel or Babylon. Almost certainly it reflects pagan influences; the names of its principal characters, the Jewish Mordechai and Esther appear to be based on the names of Babylonian gods, Marduk and Astarte.

Granted, it is the tale of how the Jewish nation is saved from impending annihilation by the political machinations of Esther and Mordechai, and no doubt by the unseen divine hand. But one has to question how it became included in the Jewish Bible. It is not a work that inspires a particular religious belief, or that conveys any great moral or ethical principles. Far from it; it seems to suggest that the Jews were saved by Esther's wily handling of her husband the king, by Mordechai's political nous, and by a great deal of luck, or possibly -and this may be the religious connection- divine intervention?

Those familiar with the Jewish Bible will immediately suspect that one reason for the appeal of the book, and its popularity, derive from a reworking of parts of the story of the much earlier biblical character Joseph. Mordechai, an exile in a foreign land, saves the Persian king's life and as a reward is led through the streets of the city by his mortal enemy Haman who is forced to proclaim 'this is what happens to the man who the king wants to honour.' Mordechai eventually rises to become prime minister of Persia. This echoes a much earlier incident in Genesis in which Joseph who has been brought to Egypt by slave traders and thrown into prison successfully interprets Pharaoh's dream, saves the king and his people from death by famine, and is consequently led in a similar fashion through the streets of Egypt, before being promoted to prime minister of Egypt. Both

Mordechai and Joseph rise from penniless refugees to become prime minister in their adopted homeland. The modelling of Mordechai's triumphal parade on that of Joseph may be intended to stress to a Jewish population who were then in exile the ethical message that with the right qualities even destitute refugees can prosper in their new homes. Equally it may be a eulogy to Hebrews who assimilate into a new culture and yet continue to remain loyal to their people and their roots.

A similar process of image creation based on well known earlier heroes could well popularise the life of Jesus in a way which served the Evangelists' purposes. And indeed we see that gospel accounts of many events in the life of Jesus mirror events that took place in the life of earlier Jewish heroes. For example, the crucifixion narrative, however real and tragic, is presented in a way which contains more than a hint of events in the life of the ancient Jewish patriarch Isaac.

From both a religious and literary perspective, the crucifixion and resurrection of Jesus is the central episode of all three synoptic gospels. Who can fail to be touched by the tragic story of the young man, betrayed by his friend, unfairly accused, scandalously tried, and then executed in the most gruesome way, all because of his beliefs? Further, who can fail to be inspired by the story of the mourners at the entrance to the tomb, the sudden appearance of an angel, the vanished body and the revelation of the resurrected Jesus? Not only is it a powerful religious narrative but it is also a dramatic piece of literature. Bearing in mind this twin mechanism, it is important to consider which of the many motifs and nuances surrounding the episode were predominantly included for theological reasons, or for the sake of historical accuracy, and which were designed to attract the attention of the listener?

The Binding of Isaac

Jesus entered Jerusalem six months before the crucifixion, riding on a donkey, a timeline confirmed by the synoptic gospels, all suggesting that the crucifixion took place at the time of the Jewish Passover.[37] But when Jesus enters Jerusalem on the donkey, Matthew records that

A very large crowd spread their cloaks on the road, while others cut branches from the trees and spread them on the road. The crowds that went ahead of him and those that followed shouted, 'Hosanna to the son of David!'[38]

The Gospel of John tells us that the branches were taken from palm trees.[39] This is a striking detail because one of the principal rituals of the Jewish festival of Succot, or Tabernacles, still performed today, is to take palm branches and walk in procession reciting hymns with the chorus line Hoshana, which means 'Oh save us.'

The procession that the crowd form with their palm branches and Hosannas to mark Jesus's entry into the city was just such a Succot procession. Succot falls in the early autumn, exactly six lunar months before Passover. From this we can surmise that Jesus entered Jerusalem six months before the crucifixion.[40]

The gospels record that Jesus's entry on a donkey was a deliberate act of theatre designed to fulfil a prophecy by the Hebrew seer Zechariah. Jesus chooses two disciples to prepare his donkey.

Now when they drew near Jerusalem, and came to Bethphage, at the Mount of Olives, then Jesus sent two disciples, saying to them, 'Go into the village opposite you, and immediately you will find a donkey tied, and a colt with her. Loose them and bring them to me. And if anyone says anything to you, you shall say. 'The Lord has need of them, and immediately he will send them.' All this was done that it might be fulfilled which was spoken by the prophet (Zechariah), saying: 'Tell the daughter of Zion, 'Behold, your king is coming to you, lowly, and sitting on a donkey, a colt, the foal of a donkey.' The disciples went and did just as Jesus directed them. They brought the donkey and the colt, laid their robes on them, and he sat on them.[41]

According to this passage from Matthew, Jesus wanted to enter Jerusalem on a donkey in order to fulfil Zechariah's prophecy. The passage from the gospel is somewhat perplexing, because it appears to suggest that Jesus was riding two donkeys simultaneously. As Geza Vermes has pointed out, the editor of Matthew is a Greek speaker and has failed to understand that the original Hebrew of Zechariah's prophecy refers to just one, not two donkeys.[42] In the parallel passages in Luke 19,35 and Mark 11,7, Jesus rides one, not two donkeys.

But if Jesus is riding just one donkey, why does he need to send two disciples to fetch it? Although this appears to be a small detail, all three synoptic gospels take the trouble to inform us specifically that Jesus sent two of them. Is there a particular reason why the gospel authors included the two disciples in this story?

Jesus's entry to Jerusalem is the beginning of a series events that will culminate in his martyrdom. The only place where the earlier Jewish literature appears to be concerned with religious martyrdom is the episode known as the Akedah, or 'the binding of Isaac', in chapter 22 of the first book of the Jewish Bible, Genesis.

In this narrative, Abraham is commanded by God to take his son Isaac and to sacrifice him. No reason is given, and the tale is presented as a test of Abraham's faith, of how far is he prepared to go for his God. It is one of the most moving and disturbing of all the Old Testament tales.

After these things, God tested Abraham. He said to him 'Abraham!' He replied, 'Here I am' He said 'Take your son, your only son, the

one you love, Isaac, and go to the land of Moriah and offer him as a
sacrifice on one of the mountains which I will show to you'.

Abraham rose early in the morning and saddled his donkey, and
took two of his young men with him, and Isaac his son; and he
chopped wood for the burnt offering, and got up and went to the
place of which God had told him. On the third day Abraham lifted
his eyes and saw the place from afar.

Abraham said to his young men, 'Stay here with the donkey;
while the boy and I go over there and pray, then we will return to
you.' So Abraham took the wood of the burnt offering and put it on
Isaac his son; and he took the fire in his hand, and the knife, and the
two of them went together.

Isaac spoke to Abraham his father and said, 'Father?' He said,
'Here I am, my son.' He said, 'Here is the fire and the wood, but
where is the lamb for a burnt offering?'

Abraham said, 'God will provide for Himself the lamb for a burnt
offering, my son.' So the two of them went together.

They came to the place of which God had told him. Abraham built
an altar there and arranged the wood and bound his son Isaac and
placed him on the altar, upon the wood. Then Abraham stretched
out his hand and took the knife to slay his son.

And an angel of God called to him from heaven and said,
'Abraham, Abraham!' He said, 'Here I am.' He said, 'Do not lay
your hand on the lad, nor do anything to him; for now I know that
you fear God, and you have not withheld your son, your only son,
from Me.' Then Abraham lifted his eyes and looked, and behold,
there was a ram, that had been caught in a thicket by its horns. So
Abraham went and took the ram, and offered it up for a burnt
offering instead of his son.[43]

In the Jewish rabbinic tradition, with which the Evangelists were
familiar, the land of Moriah to which Abraham and Isaac
journeyed was Jerusalem. That is to say, Isaac was taken by
donkey to Jerusalem, to be sacrificed. Abraham and Isaac were

accompanied on their three day journey by two young men, who were instructed to attend to the donkey. The Hebrew phrase 'young man' can mean a servant, in the same way that 'boy' can mean servant or even slave in certain English-speaking environments. According to Jewish tradition, one of these servants was the chief steward in Abraham's household,[44] who went by the name of Eliezer, and is frequently referred to as Abraham's disciple. [45]

Later in the Jewish Bible, towards the end of the Book of Numbers, we encounter the story of the heathen prophet Balaam. Balaam is a character who appears elsewhere, in ancient Middle-Eastern mythology; in 1967 an eighth century BCE, Aramaic inscription concerning Balaam was discovered at Deir 'Alla in the Jordan valley. It is unlikely that this is a Jewish inscription, but more probable that Balaam was one of a cast of prophets who featured in numerous tribal myths across the region. Nevertheless, his appearance in the Jewish Bible is his best known cameo. In his biblical role, Balaam is hired by Balak, King of Moab, to curse Israel. It takes Balak several attempts, and some generous bribes to persuade Balaam to travel to Israel's desert encampment, but he finally agrees.

And Balaam arose in the morning ... and he was riding upon his ass, with his two young men with him.[46]

As long ago as the sixth or seventh century CE the early Jewish biblical commentaries[47] recognised that elements of the Balaam narrative echoed the binding of Isaac. If Balaam is to successfully curse Israel, he will be negating the promise that God made to their progenitor Abraham, whose merit still served as a protective shield surrounding Israel. In order to penetrate this shield, Balaam needs to gain a psychological, as well as a spiritual advantage over Israel. By travelling in the same way as Abraham, on a donkey accompanied by two servants, and performing actions reminiscent of Abraham's such as rising early in the morning to saddle his own donkey, he appears to the Israelites as a new, malicious manifestation of their ancestor. This will unsettle his enemy enabling his curse to become a self-fulfilling prophecy.

Abraham travels accompanied by two servants, or disciples. Balaam, emulating Abraham does the same. Indeed the Jewish tradition deduces from these tales that anyone undertaking a journey, a dangerous enterprise in those days, should take two companions with him.

It is possible therefore that when Jesus chose to enter Jerusalem with two disciples, his travelling arrangements were a reflection of the way that things were done in those days, and a means of guaranteeing a trouble free journey. But it is more likely that the two accompanying servants or disciples in Jesus's entry into Jerusalem, mirroring Isaac's journey to the Akedah, is a deliberate motif inserted by the authors of the gospels in order to make the powerful story of the crucifixion resonate with their readership by recalling Isaac's near sacrifice.

Cloaking the crucifixion narrative in the garb of the Binding of Isaac would be a powerful literary motif. It would make an audience who had never heard of Jesus sit up and take notice; a reaction that could not be guaranteed if all they had heard was yet another ghastly report of a crucifixion- one of many judicial murders that took place daily under the Romans. It worked as a literary technique. And it was one of a number of themes that support the theory that Jesus's life history, as told in the Christian Bible, was in some way an echo of Isaac's.

Another such theme is the cross that Jesus carries.

The story of Isaac's near martyrdom recounts how the boy himself is made to carry the wood for his own pyre. The most ancient extant Jewish commentary on the biblical account notes:

So Abraham took the wood of the burnt offering and put it on Isaac his son: Like one who carries his cross on his shoulder.[48]

Jesus seems to be aware of this interpretation, for long before his crucifixion he says *to his disciples, 'If anyone would come after me, he must deny himself and take up his cross and follow me.'*[49]

This quotation from Matthew[50] occurs at the point that Jesus begins to tell his disciples that he has to go to Jerusalem, and that he will be put to death before being resurrected. It takes place prior to any suggestion that execution on the cross will play any sort of role in his story. The Romans had many forms of judicial murder at their disposal; even if Jesus did foresee his own execution, crucifixion as the means of death was not a foregone conclusion. Nevertheless Jesus specifically exhorts his followers to carry their cross, as if there is already something sacred or noteworthy either about the object itself, or about the act of carrying the implement by which one will be slaughtered.

The Via Dolorosa in the old city of Jerusalem is said to mark the route along which Jesus carried his cross to the crucifixion. Along the twisting, narrow route are fourteen stations, or sites each of which marks a particular event in the crucifixion tradition. Despite Jesus's exhortation to his followers, none of the synoptic gospels inform us that Jesus carries his own cross to the crucifixion, indeed they all introduce a passing stranger, Simon of Cyrene, who is forced by the Romans to carry Jesus's cross for him. But John, who frequently dissents from the synoptic tradition tells us that Jesus carries his own cross across the city to Golgotha, a distance of about five or six hundred metres from Pilate's court where he had been condemned.

Jesus carries the cross upon which he is to be crucified through the streets of Jerusalem just as Isaac carries the wood upon which he is to be burnt, up the mountain on which the city of Jerusalem would later be built.

Did the gospel writer- in this case John- embellish the narrative to make it correspond more closely with the binding of

Isaac? If so, why? What does Isaac symbolise which is relevant to the message the Evangelists want to tell us about Jesus?

The answer lies in the epithet 'lamb' that is used to describe both Isaac and Jesus. Religious leaders are often likened to shepherds, leading their flocks,. Indeed many of the Old Testament's prominent characters, including Jacob and Moses are shepherds. But for the leader to be designated as a lamb, the most vulnerable of the flock, is curious.

The designation of Jesus as a lamb is found twice in the Gospel of John and also in the Book of Revelations.

And looking at Jesus as He walked, he said, 'Behold the Lamb of God!'[51]

The next day John saw Jesus coming toward him, and said, 'Behold! The Lamb of God who takes away the sin of the world!'[52]

And there shall be no more curse, but the throne of God and of the Lamb shall be in it, and His servants shall serve Him.[53]

According to the Jewish Bible, Abraham hints to Isaac that when they arrive at the sacrificial site God will provide a lamb for them to sacrifice. The ancient rabbinic commentaries, however see this differently:

He (Isaac) said, 'Look, the fire and the wood, but where is the lamb for the burnt offering?' And Abraham said, 'God will see for Himself the lamb for a burnt offering, my son. [This means] God will provide a lamb for the burnt offering, and if not, you are the lamb my son.[54]

In this rabbinic expansion, the words 'my son' change from an affectionate afterthought in Abraham's reply, to an explanation that the lamb will be his son Isaac.

When this commentary was originally composed, its audience would have spotted the pun between the Greek word εσύ, meaning 'you' and the Hebrew word שׂה meaning 'lamb'. The words sound similar and by combining the Greek and Hebrew meanings the verse can be made to read *God will see for Himself, you are the lamb for a burnt offering!*[55]

To our ears it may seem strange to call somebody a lamb, and if we were to use it as an endearment, it is more about a young child, and rarely if ever regarding a grown man. Yet both Jesus and Isaac were adults.[56] So why a lamb?

By calling Jesus a lamb it seems that the Evangelists intended to draw Isaac to the attention of their readers. The idea was to fuse the identities of Isaac and Jesus in the minds of the gospel's readers so as to reinforce the idea of Jesus's crucifixion as a divine requirement.

The Resurrection

Like so much else in the literary account of Jesus's life, the seeds of his resurrection are sown in the older Hebrew bible. We have already seen how his entry into Jerusalem astride a donkey appears to echo the journey that Abraham makes to Jerusalem to obey God's command that he should sacrifice his son. We have noted that both Jesus and Isaac are referred to as lambs. They each carry their 'cross'. What we have not yet remarked upon is the association in early Jewish folk-lore of Isaac's near sacrifice with a resurrection tradition.

According to the biblical account, Isaac is saved from slaughter through the intervention of an angel.

And an angel of God called to him from heaven and said, 'Abraham, Abraham!' He said, 'Here I am.' He said, 'Do not lay your hand on the lad, nor do anything to him;'[57]

A pre-Christian tradition in Jewish literature considers Isaac to have been slaughtered and resurrected. The roots of this tradition lie in the abrupt ending to the Akedah narrative, and the subsequent unfolding of the biblical drama. After receiving the angel's blessing we read that:

Abraham returned to his young men, and they rose and went together to Beersheba; and Abraham dwelt at Beersheba.[58]

It does not require a close reading of the text to see that something is wrong. Abraham returns to his servants, and they go home. But where is Isaac? Has the narrative just overlooked him or is he truly absent?

The mystery deepens in the next chapter when Sarah, Abraham's wife and Isaac's mother, dies. We are told that Abraham buries her, but again, despite it being his mother's funeral, there is no mention of Isaac.

Isaac's reappearance into the biblical narrative is as abrupt as his disappearance. Following a lengthy episode in which Abraham's servant is sent back to his master's homeland to find a wife for Isaac, an episode in which Isaac continues to be conspicuous by his absence, we suddenly read: 'And Isaac came from the entrance to the Well-of-the-Life-That-Sees-Me.'

The disappearance of Isaac immediately after the Akedah and his reappearance at this strangely named well has fired many imaginations, with a number of legends built around it. The general theme is that Isaac is spirited away from the site of the Akedah by the angels, to recuperate from the trauma of nearly being sacrificed by his father. The name of the well then signifies his return to earthly life.

However this seems to be a sanitised version of the earlier, more sinister legend which underpins Isaac's return from the heavenly realms. The legend is ancient but continued to re-surface at times of persecution in Jewish history, in order to justify the actions of those Jews who were about to sacrifice their own lives for their faith. It is alluded to in several medieval compositions, the best known example being in a 12th CE poem describing the binding of Isaac, written by Rabbi Ephraim of

Bonn:

The resurrecting dew came down upon him and he revived. He seized him to slaughter him a second time! The Bible bears witness, the matter is attested: 'And the Lord called to Abraham a second time from the heavens.' The ministering angels cried out in terror. Even an animal is never slaughtered twice![59]

The legend even appears in the Jewish prayer book.

He lives, yet his ashes are piled up and brought before me[60]
    Appoint an advocate for me...who shall prepare the ashes of Isaac and say this is it ...[61]

Generally Judaism does do not encourage martyrdom. But this position was modified on those occasions, most notably during the crusades, when Jews were forced by marauding Christian armies in Europe to choose between conversion to the oppressor's religion, or death.

Faced with these options many Jews chose to martyr themselves and their families, rather than die a painful death at the hands of the enemy. This was a horrific option, and quite naturally they looked for role models and precedents from their religious history, in order to justify their actions.

One of the classic tales of Jewish martyrdom is recounted in the apocryphal work II Maccabees:

It also happened that seven brothers with their mother were arrested and tortured with whips and scourges by the king, to force them to eat pork in violation of God's law. One of the brothers, speaking for the others, said: 'What do you expect to achieve by questioning us? We are ready to die rather than transgress the laws of our ancestors.' At that the king, in a fury, gave orders to have pans and cauldrons heated. While they were being quickly heated, he commanded his executioners to cut out the tongue of the one who had spoken for the others, to scalp him and cut off his hands and feet, while the rest of his brothers and his mother looked on. When he was completely maimed but still breathing, the king ordered them to carry him to the fire and fry him. As a cloud of smoke spread from the pan, the brothers and their mother encouraged one another to die bravely, saying such words as these: 'The Lord God is looking on, and he truly has compassion on us...'

The tale describes in great detail how each brother is separately brought before the king, recounts their refusal to eat pork, and graphically describes their torture and death.

As the youngest brother was still alive, the king appealed to him, not with mere words, but with promises on oath, to make him rich and happy if he would abandon his ancestral customs: he would make him his friend and entrust him with high office. When the youth paid no attention to him at all, the king appealed to the mother, urging her to advise her boy to save his life. After he had urged her for a long time, she went through the motions of persuading her son. In derision of the cruel tyrant, she leaned over close to her son and said in their native language: 'Son, have pity on me, who carried you in my womb for nine months, nursed you for three years, brought you up, educated and supported you to your present age ... Do not be afraid of this executioner, but be worthy of your brothers and accept death, so that in the time of mercy I may receive you again with them.' She had scarcely finished speaking when the youth said: 'What are you waiting for? I will not obey the king's command' ... Thus he too died undefiled, putting all his trust in the Lord. The mother was last to die, after her sons.[62]

Not surprisingly, the emotive story of Hannah and her seven sons became a prototype for martyrs who were slain for their faith.

Nevertheless the Jews did not consider martyrdom to be a

religious aspiration. It remained a measure of last resort. The tale of Hannah and her seven sons was not incorporated into the Jewish Bible. Christianity however had been founded on Jesus's self-sacrifice. Martyrdom was an exalted ideal. Hannah and her sons did enter the Christian canon. The fourth century philosopher Augustine explains the reasoning for this:

> *The books of the Maccabees... are held as canonical, not by the Jews, but by the Church, on account of the extreme and wonderful sufferings of certain martyrs, who, before Christ had come in the flesh, upheld the law of God even unto death, and endured most grievous and horrible evils.*[63]

Hannah and her sons may not have made it into the Jewish Bible, but the chroniclers of Jewish martyrdom did not overlook her sacrifice. An early commentary on the book of Lamentations puts the following words into Hannah's mouth: 'You [Abraham] built one altar and did not offer up your son, but I built seven altars and offered up my sons on them.'[64] Whereas Abraham's sacrifice of his son turned out to be a trial, Hannah's was both real and sevenfold. In this way, Hannah and her sons, rather than Abraham or Isaac become the early embodiment of the Jewish martyr.

But the popularisation of the tale of Hannah did not fully excise from Jewish lore the older tradition of Isaac's martyrdom.

Ephraim of Bonn's poem was written during the time of the crusades and attests to the massacre of Jews by Christian knights. It suggests that those Jews who chose to massacre first their families and then themselves, rather than have them tortured by the enemy, used Isaac as a role model. They chose Isaac rather than Hannah's sons because as an ancestor of the nation he plays a much more central role in the eternal Jewish saga. Thus one of the most moving episodes in the Jewish Bible became a prototype of martyrdom, a religious justification for the act that they were going to commit.

The legend that Isaac was slaughtered and revived survives in other forms. Most poignantly it is associated with the second blessing of the standard Jewish prayer, Shemoneh Esreh, or Eighteen Blessings. An ancient tradition associates the three patriarchs, Abraham, Isaac, and Jacob with each of the first three blessings of this prayer. The second blessing, associated with Isaac, reads:

You are mighty for ever O Lord, reviving the dead ... .blessed are you, who revives the dead.

It appears from this that the binding of Isaac was at one time connected with a resurrection tradition, thus adding to the evidence of a conscious, thematic link between the narratives of the Akedah and the crucifixion. Particularly once we take into account the other details that the two tales have in common – the ass-laden entry into Jerusalem, the victim carrying the instrument of slaughter ,and the designation sacrificial lamb, together with the three-day context which we shall explore shortly.

3

Old Ideas, New Settings

The way that Isaac is portrayed in later Jewish legend also seems to have functioned as a prototype for the way that gospels describe Jesus's redemptive role. Jesus returns to life in order to redeem the world, his resurrection guaranteeing humanity that Jesus will again return to save them. But Jewish legend also attributed this role to Isaac, who was considered to have returned to life after having been offered as a sacrifice:

> In the future God, will say to Abraham. 'Your children have sinned against Me.' Abraham will answer: 'Sovereign of the Universe! Let them be wiped out for the sanctification of Thy Name.' Then God said "I will say this to Jacob, who experienced the pain of bringing up children: perhaps he will supplicate mercy for them. He will say to him, 'Your children have sinned.' He too shall answer 'Sovereign of the Universe! Let them be wiped out for the sanctification of Thy Name....Then shall he say to Isaac, 'Your children have sinned against me.' But Isaac shall answer him, 'Sovereign of the Universe! Are they my children and not your children?... Moreover, how much have they sinned? How many are the years of man? Seventy. Subtract the first twenty, for which you do not punish and there remain fifty. Subtract twenty-five which comprise the nights and there remain twenty-five. Subtract twelve and a half of prayer, eating, and Nature's calls, and there remain twelve and a half. If you will bear it all, let it be so; if not, let half be upon me and half upon you. And if you should say, they must all be upon me- did I not I offer myself up before you as a sacrifice[65].

The idea that Isaac plays a role as saviour is further emphasised in a short passage from the ancient commentary on the Song of Songs:

Who are the seven shepherds (mentioned in Micah 5:4)? David in the middle, Adam, Seth and Methuselah on his left, Abraham, Jacob and Moses on his right. And where did Isaac go? He went to sit at the gates of Hades, to redeem his descendants from Hell[66].

Jesus's redemptive power expands upon, but is drawn from Isaac's role as saviour. Christians will argue that the two roles are incomparable; Jesus's mission as divine saviour is far greater than anything ever claimed for Isaac. But we are looking at Jesus and Isaac from a literary perspective, not theologically. Because what we are seeing here is that the belief in a being who brings salvation from sin had already been sown in the mythology surrounding Isaac who, according to legend, had been martyred. In other words, when the Jews at whom the gospels were directed read about Jesus, they encountered an idea that was to some degree familiar, and therefore non-controversial, and thus believable; that a sacrificed hero had the power to save humanity. If it had been the first time that they had come across this idea the chances are they would not have believed it and Jesus would never have gained the prominence the Evangelists sought for him. After all the idea of Isaac as redeemer remained a fringe legend in Judaism; it was too radical to become a defining expression of Isaac's character. But by the time the Evangelists transferred this belief from Isaac to Jesus, who became the second person for whom redemptive powers were claimed, the idea was less radical, and hence more acceptable.

And it was by no means the only partially-developed theological idea that the Evangelists drew upon when seeking to describe Jesus in ways that would commend him to their Jewish readership as the latest in a long line of biblical heroes. The best known is of course the idea of Jesus as Messiah.

Messianism

Whilst Isaac may have served as the prototype for Jesus's role as saviour, Jesus's claim to messianic status is based first and foremost on an image painted by the Hebrew prophet Isaiah. In all, Christian theologians have identified dozens of prophecies in Isaiah that they believe foreshadow Jesus.[67] In particular, a whole section of Isaiah is dedicated to God's suffering servant, which appears to predict the death and resurrection of Jesus:

> *He was despised and rejected by men, a man of sorrows, and familiar with suffering. Like one from whom men hide their faces he was despised, and we esteemed him not. Surely he took up our infirmities and carried our sorrows, yet we considered him stricken by God, smitten by him, and afflicted. But he was pierced for our transgressions, he was crushed for our iniquities; the punishment that brought us peace was upon him, and by his wounds we are healed. We all, like sheep, have gone astray, each of us has turned to his own way; and the Lord has laid on him the iniquity of us all. He was oppressed and afflicted, yet he did not open his mouth; he was led like a lamb to the slaughter, and as a sheep before her shearers is silent, so he did not open his mouth.*[68]

To modern ears the title messiah is a utopian word, carrying undertones of peace, harmony, and a perfect world. But like Humpty Dumpty,[69] when moderns use a word, it means just what they choose it to mean, neither more nor less; and what people today want messiah to mean is not what the ancients intended.

The Hebrew word literally means 'anointed' and referred both to the high priest and the king, each of whom had been anointed with oil as part of their induction ceremony, a custom which is still performed today at the coronation of a British monarch. The term messiah as the title of an individual does not occur until the book of Daniel, one of the later books in the

Jewish Bible. The nearest that the early Jewish biblical tradition comes to describing a messianic figure is in the prophetic books, chiefly Isaiah and Ezekiel.

Isaiah foresees the Babylonian armies under Nebuchadnezzar invading Israel, wiping out great swathes of the population, exiling the remainder and destroying the Temple, the centre of religious life. But his core message is that there is hope in the long term; the nation will not be destroyed forever. There will be a return from exile; desolation is not eternal, God has not wholly forsaken them. The physical and spiritual restoration of the nation will be occasioned by a monarch descended from the ancient Hebrew King David. The spirit of divine wisdom will rest on him and he will rule in the fear of God with righteousness and faithfulness.[70]

Isaiah's ideal ruler will not engage in war or in the conquest of nations; weapons and the paraphernalia of war will be destroyed, and his sole concern will be to establish justice among his people.[71]

This Aquarian ideal does not stop at the restoration of national sovereignty and the establishment of a utopian society. Nature itself will change:

The wolf also shall live with the lamb, and the leopard shall lie down with the kid; and the calf and the young lion and the fatling together; and a little child shall lead them. And the cow and the bear shall feed; their young ones shall lie down together; and the lion shall eat straw like the ox. And the sucking child shall play on the hole of the asp, and the weaned child shall put his hand in the viper's den. They shall not hurt nor destroy in all my holy mountain; for the earth shall be full of the knowledge of the Lord, as the waters cover the sea. And in that day there shall be a root of Jesse, who shall stand for a banner of the people; the nations will seek him; and his tranquillity shall be glorious.[72]

Isaiah's messianic writings are the first coherent description of the perfect future, but they do not mention the word messiah, nor do they suggest that their hero is physically anointed. He would have been though, because anointing was part of a royal coronation, but it was taken for granted and had nothing other than ritual significance.

A century or so later, in the book of Ezekiel, the messianic ideal shifts away from the idea of an inspirational leader who changes the world through sheer force of personality and spirit, in favour of a more physical approach. Ezekiel, who lives in Babylon, in the midst of the captivity predicted by Isaiah, is both more militaristic, and specific in his assessment of what the messianic figure (who has still not been called 'messiah') will do. The key change in Ezekiel is that the as yet unnamed messiah is not just a figure who will usher in a period of universal harmony, he is also a warrior king who will restore political and religious independence to Israel.[73]

The title messiah emerges as *princely messiah*, in the Book of Daniel, probably written in the 3rd century BCE. The book is anachronistic, prophesying events that have already taken place. Amongst these prophecies is one that says the princely messiah will be responsible for the rebuilding of Jerusalem, which had taken place some 200 years earlier at the end of the Babylonian exile, as predicted by Isaiah and Ezekiel.

In all three cases, of Isaiah, Ezekiel, and Daniel, the messianic ideal refers to one specific act in history, the restoration of national independence following the Babylonian invasion and occupation of the country. It is applied not just to a spiritual leader who will bring perfection to the world, but to someone who is also a political and military leader, capable of leading and winning a revolution against the occupying powers. A leader descended from the stock of David, a king who first and foremost will restore national and political independence and as a direct consequence will usher in an era of peace and harmony.

Despite Daniel's prophetic hindsight the rebuilding of Jerusalem was not carried out by a princely messiah but was instead a national effort that took place over decades and was spearheaded by a succession of leaders and prophets. Although national independence was indeed restored, no all-powerful, globally acclaimed leader emerged and the idea of the messiah remained an unfulfilled dream. It resurfaced from time to time at moments of national crisis, but did not emerge again in full force until the time of a much later military trauma, the invasion by Rome in the 1st century BCE.

As the title 'messiah' resurfaces in the popular vocabulary during Roman times it goes through yet another change. For those who seek political freedom from Rome, the utopian ideal disappears, as does the need for the messiah to be descended from King David. The messiah remains nothing more than a military leader who will defeat Rome in battle and drive them from the land. This is how the Jews saw Bar Koziba, who led the most successful of his nation's many revolts against Rome. Between 132 and 135 CE his rebels managed to establish an independent state, resisting the Roman military might. It is clear that he enjoyed the support of the Jewish religious establishment. Rabbi Akiva, an outstanding sage and the undisputed religious leader of the Bar Koziba generation refers to him as 'King Messiah'[74] and he becomes known popularly as Bar Kochba meaning 'son of the star', an allusion to Balaam's messianic prophecy in Numbers 24,17.[75]

By the time of Jesus therefore, two parallel concepts of messiah exist. Jesus himself, whose ancestry is traced in the gospels back to David, fits the model of spiritual leader, whilst Bar Koziba represents the warrior-king, national liberator. The two are worlds apart, yet exist side-by-side.

The idea that David is the progenitor of the messiah is not found in the biblical stories about him. It starts with Isaiah, some 400 years later, and is based to a large degree on an idealised, mythical David who had none of the human flaws of the real king. But despite his weaknesses, described at length in the Book of Samuel, the David stories do single him out for special treatment. He becomes only the second king of Israel, and the first to establish a dynasty, having seized power from his former mentor Saul. On one hand, he is portrayed as a sensitive musician yet a mighty warrior, a just leader and a much wronged father. But on the other he is shown to be a jealous adulterer, sending the husband of his paramour to his death in battle, as well as being a ruthless, if successful, warlord.

In part, the dream that the Davidic line will be restored is nothing more than a yearning for a renewal of the national identity and independence that was lost when Babylon conquered Israel in the 6th century BCE and brought David's royal line to an end. David was never formally acclaimed as a messiah in his lifetime, because the concept did not exist in his day. But he could have been, since he displayed both the military and religious leadership necessary to fulfil this role: Militarily, not only did his armies finally defeat the Philistines, who had been a constant enemy of Israel, they also subjugated several other neighbouring tribes, thereby extending the borders of the land to a previously undreamed of horizon. Religiously, he is named as author of half of the sonnets in the book of Psalms, and indirectly credited as having written the remainder. He regains the ark of the covenant from the Philistines who had stolen it some decades earlier and draws up plans to establish a permanent central place of worship in his capital, Jerusalem, which he has recently captured from the Jebusite nation. God however thwarts his plans, telling him that he has shed too much blood to be permitted to build a permanent house of worship.[76]

Jesus's direct descent from David is spelt out in the gospels[77] and this together with his spiritual credentials will establish his claim to messianic status. But shortly we will see that he too is not the only messianic candidate to figure in the gospels. The other will be identified by approaching our reading of the gospels with an eye to its hidden agenda. But before then we have other emerging theological ideas, developed by the gospels, to consider.

Three Days

We saw that Isaac and Abraham travelled for three days to the site where Isacc was to be bound and sacrifices. And of course three days elapses between the crucifixion of Jesus and the resurrection. The three day theme, which recurs in several places in both bibles provides powerful evidence of the literary dependence of the gospels upon the Old Testament.

Jesus took the Twelve aside and told them, "We are going up to Jerusalem, and everything that is written by the prophets about the Son of Man will be fulfilled. He will be handed over to the Gentiles. They will mock him, insult him, spit on him, flog him and kill him. On the third day he will rise again."[78]

The three-day period that elapsed between Jesus's crucifixion and resurrection represents a fundamental pillar of Christianity, and Jesus himself specifically predicts that he will rise again after three days.[79] This interval, that now defines the duration of the Easter period, however, is by no means the only three-day period in the Christian Bible.

A three-day interval occurs in the well-known episode of the loaves and fishes, when a hungry crowd have had no food for three days:

Now Jesus called his disciples and said, 'I have pity on the multitude, because they have now continued with me three days and have nothing to eat. And I do not want to send them away hungry, lest they faint on the way.' Then his disciples said to him, 'Where could we get enough bread in the wilderness to fill such a great multitude?' Jesus said to them, 'How many loaves do you have?' And they said, 'Seven, and a few little fish.' So he commanded the multitude to sit down on the ground. And he took the seven loaves and the fish and gave thanks, broke them and gave them to his disciples; and the disciples gave to the multitude. [80]

And, in what may be a literary pre-figuring of the resurrection narrative, because it is the first occasion that Jesus returns to his loved ones, he is separated from his parents for three days. We are not told where he has been, only where he was found:

...As they returned, the boy Jesus lingered behind in Jerusalem ... when they did not find him, they returned to Jerusalem, seeking him. Now so it was that after three days they found him in the Temple, sitting in the midst of the teachers, both listening to them and asking them questions[81]

The three-day period is also found regularly in the Hebrew Bible. We first see it in Genesis when Joseph interprets the dreams of Pharaoh's butler and baker, who are in prison with him. The baker has dreamt of three baskets of bread, the butler of a three-branched grape vine. Joseph tells them that in each case they symbolise three days. In three days time the butler is to have his life spared and the baker is to hang.

Later, in the Book of Exodus, as part of the long and tortuous negotiations to have the Hebrew nation freed from slavery, Moses asks Pharaoh to allow the Israelites to go on a three-day journey in the wilderness, to sacrifice to God. The Book of Jubilees, a reconstruction of the early bible stories written in pre-Christian times by a Jewish sect who adhered to a solar calendar, explains that this was to celebrate a festival that Abraham had instituted to commemorate Isaac's near sacrifice.

Forty years on, when the Israelites finally enter the land of Israel after the death of Moses, their leader Joshua sends spies out into the Canaanite city of Jericho. The local chiefs get wind of their presence and the spies are forced to hide for three days until they know it is safe to return to the camp.

In the book of Esther, Haman, the Prime Minister of Persia persuades King Ahasuerus that the Jews should be wiped out. Upon hearing the news, Esther, Ahasuerus's Jewish wife commands her people to fast with her for three days, before she begs an audience with the king.

And when Jonah flees in a ship from Jaffa to try to avoid the mission that God has sent him upon, the boat is overtaken by a storm and he is thrown overboard. He is swallowed by a giant fish, in whose belly he remains for three days before being spewed up, alive on dry land.

In these, and many other biblical instances, three days symbolises a period of physical or spiritual preparation leading to liberation or the saving of life. As Hosea sums it up:

He will revive us after two days, and on the third day He will raise us up so we can live in His presence.[82]

In a Christian context, Matthew puts it as follows:

For as Jonah was in the belly of the great fish three days and three nights, so the Son of Man will be in the heart of the earth three days and three nights.[83]

The three days that elapsed between crucifixion and resurrection was predicted by Jesus but this was no whim. It was recorded in the gospels because it was theologically necessary. It conformed to Hosea's prophecy, and fitted into the ancient Jewish concept that three days was a necessary interval between destruction and resurgence. The three-day theme in the crucifixion narrative is almost certainly carried forward from the Hebrew Bible, and is another indication of the literary dependence of the New

Testament upon the Old.

Virgin Birth

We are suggesting that those for whom the gospels were written would have been familiar with many of its key concepts- that in effect the gospels fitted into a world view which was already emerging.

Mary's virginity is one of those topics which is understated in the gospels but which rises in the fullness of time to much greater prominence. Mary is referred to as a virgin by both Luke[84] and Matthew[85] but the theological implications are not fully developed until long after the gospels are written. Nevertheless, the idea of virgin birth was already being discussed in Jewish circles some time before the gospels were written.

Three and a half centuries before the birth of Jesus, the Macedonian emperor Alexander the Great began his conquest of the then-known world. This was the start of the largest fusion of nations and peoples the world had ever seen, with the cross-fertilisation of cultures taking place at a phenomenal rate. It was also an unparalleled upheaval of the old world. We have seen in our own times how TV, cinema, and the internet have helped to create a homogenous, global culture, but this is not the first time it happened. The ancient world may not have had electronic and visual media, but what they did have was people of every creed and race crossing borders and entering cities as slaves, soldiers, merchants, and bureaucrats.

Over the ensuing centuries conquest, empire, and trade continued to erase the boundaries between different tribes and lands, creating a melting pot of societies, centred on the Mediterranean but extending to northern Europe at one extreme, north Africa to the south and as far as the Arabian deserts in the east.

The Romans, with their superior technology and military

reach accelerated this merging of societies. Their architecture and engineering may have transformed the way people lived their daily lives, but whatever advantages and traumas the Romans brought to their subjects, it was not all one-way traffic. Technological advances, such as aqueducts and heated bath houses flowed out of Rome, new ideas streamed into it. The Roman pantheon found itself challenged by the more sophisticated Eastern theologies. The Egyptian gods Isis and Osiris reached Rome at the beginning of the first century BCE, and the cult of the Persian sun god Mithras a century later. The new concept of Monotheism threatened the traditional Roman gods, initially through Stoicism, which was the first discipline to introduce the concept of a single god and later due to Gnostic and Jewish influences. The Roman people were ready for greater intellectual challenges; Jewish sources of the period are replete with tales of Roman dignitaries, and particularly Roman women, anxious to learn new ideas, to be exposed to a more sophisticated level of religious belief.

Several of these Roman women, known in Jewish literature as *matronas* appear to have been well-versed in the Jewish Bible and took an active interest in quizzing the rabbis of their day about its apparent contradictions or inconsistencies. They were familiar with the biblical texts, and able to quote from them.

Most of the debates that have come down to us took place in the second century between one or more of these women, and Rabbi Yose bar Halafta:

A matrona said to Rabbi Yose, 'My god is greater than yours.' He asked 'Why?' 'Because when your God appeared to Moses at the burning bush, Moses hid his face. But when he saw the snake, which is my god, he ran away.'[86]

A matrona asked Rabbi Yose barHalafta, 'Why was Esau born first (before his twin brother Jacob)?'[87]

A matrona asked Rabbi Yose bar Halafta, 'How can it be that

Joseph, a seventeen-year-old boy at the peak of his sexual powers, resisted the sexual advances of his mistress? [88]

The *matronas* were part of the Roman elite, probably the wives of state officials. They did not just have the time on their hands to take an interest in the culture of the countries to which their husbands had been posted, they also had sufficient education to learn new languages, and to read and understand the local literature. These women were also sufficiently self-possessed to dispute the domestic cultural and religious assumptions. Although Jewish literature records the refutations that the rabbis gave to their challenges, it is the questions these women pose which tell us more about the cross-cultural mix in those days, than the responses of the rabbis.

A matrona asked Rabbi Yose bar Halafta, 'How many days did God spend creating his world?' He answered: 'Six, as we know from the verse, "For in six days God created the heavens and the earth." [89] *'And what.' asked she 'has he been doing since then?' 'He sits and matches couples – this woman's daughter to this man's son.' 'That is his occupation?' she snorted. 'I can do that. Look how many servants I have, men and women. In a quick hour I could pair them all up.' He replied, 'It might be a light thing in your eyes. In God's eyes it is as great a task as parting the Red Sea.'* [90]

A matrona asked Rabbi Yose bar Halafta, 'Why does the Bible say "He gives wisdom to the wise."? [91] *Surely it should say He gives wisdom to those who are not wise!'* [92]

Israel, or Judea as the Romans called it stood at a geographical crossroads in the Roman empire. The King's Highway, the main trade route from Egypt to Syria passed along its western edge. The *Via Maris* or Way of the Sea was the coastal route that carried people, goods, and ideas from Pelesium in Egypt to Damascus. The Spice Route led up from the Persian Gulf, crossing both the

Kings Highway and the *Via Maris* on its way to the coast at Gaza.

Amongst the many tales, fables, and stories that were recounted by those traversing the ancient highways, were the legends and myths of diverse cultures. Alexander the Great's armies would have brought with them the adventures of the Greek pantheon, prominent amongst which was the birth of Heracles, or Hercules. Fathered by Zeus, the chief of the Greek gods, Hercules had a human mother, Alcmene. Zeus's dalliance with a mortal woman enraged his wife, the goddess Hera. To try to calm her, Alcmene named the child after her. This only angered her further, and matters were made worse when Zeus bestowed eternal life upon the baby Hercules by placing him at Hera's breast whilst she slept.

The raconteurs in the ancient caravans and armies that travelled on these roads would have known many such tales, of wondrous births, miraculous babies who achieved great things, and of gods who mated with humans. Romulus and Remus, founders of the city of Rome, born out of the rape of their human mother, Rhea Silvia, by the god Mars and raised by wolves; the prophet Zoroaster who laughed on the day of his birth; and the Egyptian god Horus who was born when his mother Isis, having assumed the shape of a bird, discovered the dead body of her husband Osiris. Fanning the air with her wings she drew Osiris's essence into herself and conceived Horus.

How would this constant mingling of traditions over many centuries influence the literary and cultural traditions of the Jews? The ancient Jewish concept of the land of Israel as the centre of the world was not just a self important national myth. They viewed themselves as sitting at the centre of the world because of the many different nationalities and races that passed through their borders. Living at this busy junction of the ways, the Jews could not have remained ignorant of the many cultural currents that traversed their lands. Even their Bible, whose early chapters are dedicated to rational explanations of the wonders of existence did not remain immune to fables concerning wondrous, unnatural births:

> *So it was that when men began to multiply on the face of the earth and daughters were born to them, that the sons of God saw that the daughters of men were attractive, and they took wives from whomsoever they chose for themselves ... The fallen ones were on the earth on those days, and even after, when the sons of God came upon the daughters of men, who bore children to them ...*[93]

The idea that 'the sons of God' could mate with human women and could father children, is theologically outrageous. The Jewish Bible is largely matter-of-fact in the way it portrays events. Granted, there are miracles, and of course the literature demands that its readers believe in God if they are to fully engage with it, but most of its tales and narratives are about human or natural events, not about super-beings arriving on earth and ravishing its women. But in fact, this is just the tip of the iceberg. For over and over again, we see hints in the Old Testament of a divine-human marriage, not between the sons of God and women, but between God himself, and the people of Israel.

For example, the Hebrew word which means 'to know' can be used in a sexual as well as an intellectual sense. Carnal knowledge. *And Adam knew Eve his wife and she conceived ...*[94] means that Adam and Eve had sexual relations. Similarly, when the prophet Hosea talks about God betrothing Israel to him, and Israel knowing God, there is little doubt that this too is physical imagery:

> *And I shall betroth you to me for ever, and I shall betroth you to me in righteousness and justice and kindness and mercy and I shall betroth you to me in faith, and you shall know the Lord.*[95]

Ezekiel takes this imagery even further. As part of a long passage decrying the behaviour of ancient Israel, and portraying their origins in the most abject terms, he compares the nation to an unfaithful wife:[96]

And I passed by you and looked upon you and behold your time was the time of love, and I spread my garment over you and I covered your nakedness and I promised to you and entered into a covenant with you says the Lord, and you were mine. I clothed you with embroidery, and I made precious skins for your shoes, I wound fine linen upon your head and covered you with silk. I decked you with ornaments and put bracelets on your hands and a necklace upon your throat... but you trusted in your beauty, and you played the whore... The difference between you and other women is that you were the seducer and were not seduced by another, and that you paid those with whom you committed whoredom and they did not pay you.[97]

Any suggestion in the Jewish Bible of a mystical, sexual relationship between God and humankind, is never anything more than that, a suggestion, a mere hint, a twinkle in the eye. We can understand this in one of two ways. Either the idea is too daring, too outrageous to be spelled out in full, or as a concept it is still in its earliest stages, an undeveloped seed that will gestate in the fullness of time, in the post-biblical age. Given the Jewish Bible lack of inhibition regarding carnal matters and its predilection for graphic, physical and sexual imagery, the latter hypothesis seems more likely. Influenced probably by other cultures, the Jewish Bible hints at a physical relationship between God and his people but is reluctant to take the idea further, leaving it as a tantalising concept to be fully developed in the esoteric realms, as indeed the kabbalists did many centuries later.

So we have the hints in Genesis, and we also have a resurgence of the idea, in a slightly more developed, but still largely undefined way in the books of the prophets. The idea of *unio mystica*, a mystical union, does not become fully developed until the later books of the Jewish Bible. Particularly, in several books which fall into a category known as Wisdom literature.

Wisdom literature is not specifically Jewish. It seems to have emerged in the ancient near east, especially in Egypt and Mesopotamia. As trade and cultures spread and cross-fertilised throughout the near east, Wisdom literature extended its appeal. One branch found its way into Jewish thought, crystallising in biblical books such as Proverbs and Ecclesiastes, the apocryphal Ben Sira and in the Wisdom of Solomon, amongst others. Wisdom was an important motif and concept in Jewish philosophical writings in the centuries before Jesus.

Wisdom introduces itself in the Book of Proverbs:

The Lord possessed me at the beginning of His way, before His works of old. I have been established from everlasting, from the beginning, before there was ever an earth. When there were no depths I was brought forth, when there were no fountains abounding with water. Before the mountains were settled, before the hills, I was brought forth. While as yet He had not made the earth or the fields, or the primeval dust of the world. When He prepared the heavens, I was there, when He drew a circle on the face of the deep, when He established the clouds above, when He strengthened the fountains of the deep. When He assigned to the sea its limit, so that the waters would not transgress His command, when He marked out the foundations of the earth, then I was beside Him as a master craftsman. And I was daily His delight, rejoicing always before Him, rejoicing in His inhabited world, and my delight was with the sons of men.[98]

These verses cast Wisdom as a pre-existent being, partner with God in creation. Mainstream Jewish tradition holds that the above verses apply, not to Wisdom as a concept, but specifically to the Torah, the sacred, religious teaching of the Jews, encapsulated in the Five Books of Moses. We are using the word Wisdom deliberately however, because this is how the passage is understood by the Greek-Jewish philosopher Philo of Alexandria, who was active at the beginning of the Christian era, and whose interpretation of virgin birth is relevant to our investigation.

Wisdom in the book of Proverbs is a spiritual entity, a craftsman used by God in the creation of the world. Many years later by the time the Wisdom of Solomon is written, sometime between 50 BCE and 50 CE, Wisdom has taken on a feminine character, as a bride of God:

For Wisdom is mobile beyond all motion, and she penetrates and pervades all things by reason of her purity... And passing into holy souls from age to age, she produces friends of God and prophets. ... I loved her and sought her from my youth, and I desired to take her for my bride, and I became enamoured of her beauty. She glorifies her noble birth by living with God, and the Lord of all loves her. For she is an initiate in the knowledge of God, and an associate in his works.[99]

Although the Wisdom of Solomon does not tell us how God's pure bride produces 'friends of God and prophets' it does say that 'She glorifies her noble birth by living with God.' The Greek word is *symbiosin*, literally living together. We can turn to Philo of Alexandria to develop the idea further:

God is ... the husband of Wisdom, sowing for the race of mankind the seed of happiness in good and virgin soil.[100]

At all events we shall speak with justice, if we say that the Creator of the universe is also the father of his creation; and that the mother was the Wisdom of the Creator with whom God uniting, not as a man unites, became the father of creation. And this Wisdom, having received the seed of God, when the day of her travail arrived, brought forth her only and well-beloved son, perceptible by the external senses, namely this world.[101]

Philo, an Egyptian Jew who was an older contemporary of Jesus is the only remaining alumnus of a philosophical school whose literature which is now lost. He is aware of a sacred union between God and the female Wisdom, as a result of which an only son is born. Some scholars, influenced by WF Albright[102] who saw a Canaanite background to the book of Proverbs, believe that Wisdom herself is a personification of a female Canaanite goddess.[103] Theories abound that the virgin Mary symbolises a repressed mother goddess cult, with its roots in the Egyptian goddess Isis, which found an outlet within Christianity.[104]

We cannot prove anything by invoking speculative theories, and we can only surmise how widely the idea of virgin birth had entered Jewish theological thought by the time that Christianity emerged. Nevertheless we can see that the idea of a sacred marriage between God and a virgin bride, giving birth to an only son, was not wholly unknown in Judaism, at least several decades before the birth of Jesus. So it is reasonable to assume that, far from being an idea that was so radical and shocking that it convincingly asserted a new truth, Mary's virginity was a radically acceptable and reassuringly edgy motif, which made it easier for the stories being told about Jesus to be accepted into Jewish society.

So we can see how both Jewish bible heroes and philosophical ideas current in the decades before, and during Jesus's life are likely to have had an influence on the composition of the gospels. The question of course is, so what? This book began by referring to a failed rebellion which is concealed between the lines in the gospels. What I am trying to suggest now is that by looking in more detail at the influences that Jewish literature had on the composition of the gospels we will be in a much better position to be able to discern the agenda that is concealed beneath their narrative. An agenda of which the failed rebellion was to have been a central event.

4

Greater than Moses

When attempts at systematic and scientific, literary criticism began in the nineteenth century much attention was paid to parallels between biblical literature and the myths of other civilisations. There are copious examples of resemblances between stories in the Jewish Bible and older, external works. The Epic of Gilgamesh, written four thousand years ago, contains a tale of a flood which devastates mankind. Its hero Uta-napishti builds a boat, places all his possessions in it and rides out the storm. When the waters abate he sends out a dove, which returns to him, then a raven which does not come back. In the Jewish account, Noah saves himself from the flood by building a boat, universally though inexplicably known as an ark. When the rains cease he sends out, first a raven, which flies to and fro, then a dove which returns with an olive branch in its mouth.

The Mesopotamian ruler, Sargon of Akkad is known to us from legends inscribed on cuneiform tablets over a two thousand year period. Sargon comes from humble origins, his father is unknown although his mother may have been a priestess. An Assyrian text, probably from the seventh century BCE describes his origins:

My mother was a changeling, my father I knew not. The brothers of my father loved the hills. My city is Azupiranu, which is situated on the banks of the Euphrates. My changeling mother conceived me, in secret she bore me. She set me in a basket of rushes, with bitumen she sealed my lid. She cast me into the river which rose over me. The river bore me up and carried me to Akki, the drawer of water. Akki, the drawer of water, took me as his son and reared me. Akki, the drawer of water, appointed me as his gardener. While I was a gardener, Ishtar granted me her love, and for four and [...] years I exercised kingship[105].

Sargon is found as a baby, floating in a basket on a river. From such an unpropitious start, he rapidly rises through ancient Mesopotamian society to become its king, ultimately defeating Lugalzaggisi of Erech whose kingdom stretches from the Mediterranean to Elam, in the southwest of modern Iran. Sargon lived around 2,300 BCE. This places him nearly a thousand years before Moses, whose mother, unable to raise him because of Pharaoh's decree that all the baby boys are to be drowned, put him into a basket, sealed it with bitumen and placed him in the rushes at the side of the river. Which was where Pharaoh's daughter found him, and then took him to her father's palace and raised him as her son.

These, and many other reformulations of ancient tales are iconic stories, the foundation of national myths, and the under-pinnings of cultural identity. They appear to be part of a chain of narrative stretching across centuries and cultures.

And just as the narrative elements of the Moses drama appear to have been drawn from earlier works in other cultures, so too we will see a connection between Jesus and Moses. In which Moses, whilst remaining the Jewish prototype of the ideal religious leader, becomes in literary terms a stepping stone in a continuous literary tradition stretching out over two and half, ancient millennia.

Association and Dissociation

Moses was universally acknowledged by the Jews as their greatest leader. The five books attributed to him remain, even today, the pre-eminent work of Jewish religious and legal liter-ature. His act in bringing the Jews out of slavery in Egypt had brought political independence to the nation. When the Bible recounts that God personally dictated the Ten Commandments and the rest of the Torah to Moses on Mount Sinai the Jewish faith was born. Moses was liberator, law giver and spiritual leader, when the people spoke of him simply as 'Moses our teacher' this was because no other epithet could fully encompass all his qualities.

Understandably, the gospels go to great lengths to disassociate themselves from the heritage that Moses gave to the Jews. It is this disassociation, more than anything else that indicates a break with the past, and a new beginning. It is not at all surprising that the gospels contain passages which stress that the new Christians had progressed beyond the towering figure who dominated the Jewish faith for over a thousand years:

The law of Moses and the writings of the prophets were preached until John came. Since then, the Good News about the kingdom of God is being told. [106]
The law of Moses could not free you from your sins. But through Jesus everyone who believes is free from all sins. [107]

But the disassociation could not be absolute. One cannot encourage a mass population to accept new ideas by tearing up the beliefs they have held sacred up to that point. One of the challenges that faced the gospel authors would have been how to portray Jesus in a way which both built on the foundations that Moses had laid, whilst elevating him beyond this. All the prophets of the Jewish Bible had recast Moses's essential message in terms which spoke to their generations. Jesus's followers aspired to transcend this, to establish a new religious vocabulary, yet one which still resonated with the people amongst whom they lived.

Many of the key events in Jesus's life take place on mountains. He delivers the sermon on the mount, [108] heals a leper as he comes down from an unidentified mountain, [109] descends from yet another mountain to walk upon water, [110] heals the lame, crippled, and blind on a promontory overlooking the Sea of Galilee,[111] and appears resurrected to his disciples upon the same mountain.[112]

Likewise, Moses also experiences his greatest moments upon mountain tops. His first divine revelation occurs at the burning bush on Mount Horeb, [113] he receives God's Torah, upon Mount Sinai, [114] and during his two forty-day periods of fasting upon the mountain, is afforded a vision of God's presence. [115] Although Moses leads the Israelites through the hilly wilderness, Jesus lives in a land which, despite having some scattered mountains, is by no means mountainous country. The Galilee where much of Jesus's life is set contains plains, forests, and seas. But it is mountains that figure prominently in both their stories.

At the end of his life, Moses ascends Mount Nebo at God's command, climbing the summit known as Pisgah. Mount Nebo lies in the dusty mountains of Moab, in the modern state of Jordan, to the east of Jericho. Pisgah and its neighbouring summits stand at the south-eastern edge of the biblical land of Israel. They afford a panoramic view of the tiny country, northwards along the length of the River Jordan which flows far beneath sea level from the hills of Galilee with its inland sea, past Jericho southwards, to the sites of the destroyed cities of Sodom and Gomorrah. Westward the view is over the Judean hills to the Mediterranean. Moses is told to climb to the top of Nebo in order to gaze out over the promised land[116] to which he has brought his people, but which he himself is forbidden to enter. This represents the great tragedy of Moses's life – the leader who brought a slave nation out of Egypt and led them through the wilderness for forty years towards a promised land, is destined only to glimpse it from afar and never to enter therein. As Moses views the promised land he sees not just its geographical contours and physical outline, but also its future history unfurled before him.

In contrast, the Christian Bible contains what might be

considered to be a parody on this episode. At the very beginning of his mission and immediately after being baptised, Jesus is taken into the wilderness by the devil. After fasting for forty days and forty nights (exactly as Moses had done on two occasions) [117] the devil takes him to the top of a high mountain and shows him all the kingdoms of the world and their glory. [118] Thus here we have, the beginning of his mission, rather than the end; the devil and not God; the nations of the world and not Israel. The one nation focus that Moses has is replaced by Jesus's universalistic outlook; the promise that God makes to Moses is countered by the devil's boast to Jesus of the world's temptations.

Moses was born at a time when Pharaoh, ruler of Egypt, had decreed that all the Jewish baby boys were to be killed. Herod, ruler of Israel, having heard of the birth of Jesus sought to kill him. Herod's decree was specifically against the infant Jesus whereas the biblical account implies that Moses just happened to be born at a bad time for Jewish babies. Until we consider this Talmudic parable:

Pharaoh's astrologers saw that Israel's liberator would be destroyed through water: therefore he ordered 'Every son that is born ye shall cast into the river' (Exodus 1,22). But the astrologers did not know that Moses's death would be brought about by events at the water of Meribah. [119]

This homily tells us that Pharaoh's decree to drown the baby boys was specifically intended to get rid of Moses, just as Herod's decree was aimed at Jesus. The waters of Meribah were where Moses disobeyed God's command, as a consequence of which it was decreed that he would die in the wilderness and not enter the promised land. Moses death therefore was indeed brought about by water. Unfortunately for Pharaoh, although his astrologers got the method of Moses's death right; they got the place and time wrong.

Having failed to find the child Jesus, Herod emulates Moses's Pharaoh and decrees a sentence of death upon all the infant boys:

Then Herod, when he saw that he was deceived by the wise men, was exceedingly angry; and he sent forth and put to death all the male children who were in Bethlehem and in all its districts, from two years old and under. [120]

In the Moses narrative, a new born child poses a threat to a mighty ruler, leading to an assault on the infant's life. When it becomes clear that the baby will not be found, the king attempts to wipe out all the children of a similar age.

The same structure appears in the Jesus narrative. Failing to track down the infant Jesus, Herod decrees death to all male babies. In the Moses narrative, we may suspect that the story was inspired by one or more legends drawn from an external culture, or even possibly that there was a pre-existing proto-myth that inspired all similar stories. In Hindu mythology, Kansa has failed in his attempts to prevent the birth of Krishna, who, he has been warned, will one day kill him. He tries to ensure that the baby does not survive, by ordering the killing of all babies born in the past ten days. Of course he fails to find the baby.

But the Jesus narrative emanates from a society familiar with the Moses story, and so it is unlikely that the same process of cross-cultural fertilisation from external sources was at work. It is also unlikely that the gospel scribes did not spot the similarity between their tale and that of Moses; which leaves us with the probability that this aspect of the Jesus story was specifically written to evoke Moses in the mind of the reader.

In order to escape Herod's soldiers, Mary, Joseph, and their infant son flee to Egypt. In a contrasting fashion Moses flees from Egypt, having slain an Egyptian taskmaster whom he caught abusing a fellow Israelite. Both Jesus and Moses eventually return to their homeland when they receive a divine message.

Interestingly, Matthew uses exactly the same phrase as the Jewish Bible to describe the message. In the Jewish bible we read of Moses:

For all the men who sought your life are dead. [121]

In Matthew we find of Jesus:

For all who sought the young child's life are dead. [122]

The similarity of language, as well as the details in the narrative reinforce the idea of a deliberate parallel between the accounts of the early life of both Jesus and Moses.

To recap: we have seen that elements of Jesus's life story, as recounted in the gospels are based on the exploits of earlier, Old Testament heroes, particularly Moses and Isaac.

We have also suggested that the gospel writers were trying to communicate something to their audience over and above Jesus's religious teachings. That beneath the surface of the gospel narrative lies a suppressed agenda – one which was far less obscure at the time it was written than now. It is this agenda which sets Jesus's spiritual teachings in context.

To get beneath the surface of the gospel narratives and understand the political message that the Evangelists were trying to communicate to their first century Jewish audience, we need to read the gospels in the same way that their audience would. Jewish Bible stories were rarely taken at mere face value, alongside the bare narrative there would lie layers of interpretations and explanations. These interpretations may have had a legal, ethical, religious or mythical dimension to them. But they were all derived using a common set of interpretative rules; we can think of these rules as formal techniques for reading between the lines. By understanding a little of how these rules worked we can start to see how the Jewish Bible was decoded by those who read or taught it. And we can start to apply the same code breaking techniques to the gospels.

5

Decoding the Bible

Arguably, what we have seen in the previous chapters is the development of a cultural tradition, the propagation, by Jews, of fundamental Jewish mythic narratives into the new arena of Christianity. Christianity began its life as a Jewish sect, and it is reasonable to expect it to hold fast to mainstream Jewish ideas motifs and patterns. One of which is to carry literary connections forward into a continuous thread that weaves its way through diverse compositions composed over an extended period of time.

Living at a time when Christianity was in its infancy, and with no interest in establishing connections between it and their own Jewish faith, the ancient rabbinic exegetes, or bible commentators, confined their interpretative techniques to the Jewish Bible. Yet their methodology, known as Midrash can be extrapolated to draw comparisons between the Hebrew and Christian Bibles, which emerged from a common culture, and which as we have seen, have literary features in common. We have already used midrashic techniques to identify the influence of earlier biblical character portraits upon the literary image of Jesus as portrayed in the gospels, and to hypothesise as to what the significance of these connections may be.

We have seen that Jesus is portrayed as the latest in a long line of Jewish religious leaders, a man whose spiritual and leadership characteristics were drawn from well established and deeply respected sources. Midrash provides us with insights into Jesus's mission, and into the religious ideas that can be derived from a study of the biblical account of his life.

But most importantly, it allows us to gather historical evidence about Jesus the man and the agenda that he and his disciples had. Evidence which is woven into the Gospel narrative, but which is not immediately apparent unless we understand the literary devices that the evangelists, the authors of the gospels, used. Evidence which is concealed, for example, in the account of the Transfiguration, the narrative of the crucifixion and the brief history of Barabbas.

The Transfiguration

The separate histories of the Old Testament Moses and the New Testament Jesus converge when the two spiritual giants meet at the Transfiguration, one of the most difficult of all gospels passages to understand.

After six days Jesus took with him Peter, James and John the brother of James, and led them up a high mountain by themselves. There he was transfigured before them. His face shone like the sun, and his clothes became as white as the light. Just then there appeared before them Moses and Elijah, talking with Jesus. Peter said to Jesus, "Lord, it is good for us to be here. If you wish, I will put up three shelters—one for you, one for Moses and one for Elijah." While he was still speaking, a bright cloud enveloped them, and a voice from the cloud said, "This is my Son, whom I love; with him I am well pleased. Listen to him!" When the disciples heard this, they fell face down to the ground, terrified. But Jesus came and touched them. "Get up," he said. "Don't be afraid." When they looked up, they saw no one except Jesus. As they were coming down the mountain, Jesus instructed them, "Don't tell anyone what you have seen, until the Son of Man has been raised from the dead." The disciples asked him, "Why then do the teachers of the law say that Elijah must come first?" Jesus replied, "To be sure, Elijah comes and will restore all things. But I tell you, Elijah has already come, and they did not recognize him... [123]

The gospels make no mention of what transpired in the conversation between Moses, Elijah and Jesus. But in each gospel we find the same the sequence of events: Jesus and his disciples climb a mountain whereupon his clothes and physical appearance alter. Moses and Elijah appear and converse with him, Peter offers to make shelters, a heavenly voice proclaims Jesus to be the son of God, Moses and Elijah each disappear and the disciples are sworn to secrecy.

We already know that Jesus and Moses share a literary affinity. But what of Elijah? Where has he come from and why does he turn up in this story? If we look more closely at the biblical accounts of each of them we can discover common threads between each of the characters, and at least one of the others, establishing a threefold link between them.

Elijah first appears in the biblical book of Kings, some one hundred years after David and a little less than a century before Isaiah.[124] He ascends to heaven in a fiery chariot[125] and according to Jewish tradition remains immortal, wandering the earth in the guise of an old man, performing miracles, assisting those in despair and distress. But alongside his role as a friend to the needy, Elijah is also a central figure in the drama that will take place, according to Jewish lore, at the end of days. A rabbinic teaching, based on a verse in the biblical book of Malachi is that Elijah will herald the coming of the messiah:

Behold, I will send you Elijah the prophet before the coming of the great and dreadful day of the Lord. [126]

We might surmise from the brief account of the Transfiguration that Moses is teaching Jesus something, advising him, or even inducting him into office. Or that he is passing on his mantle. (The English phrase to pass on a mantle comes from the account of the death of Elijah, when he ascends to heaven in a fiery chariot and casts his robe, or mantle, over his successor Elisha.[127]) Alternatively, perhaps Moses is paying homage. The leader whose law was declared to be superseded has descended from the heavens, so to speak, in order to subordinate himself to Jesus. Elijah's presence would then presumably be to confirm Jesus as the messiah, the ancient Hebrew prophet consulting with him prior to proclaiming his coming, as predicted in the Old Testament book of Malachi.

But this is snookered by the fact that immediately after the Transfiguration Jesus tells his disciples that Elijah has effectively already proclaimed the Messiah, but that the world failed to take notice.

Both Elijah and Moses experience their greatest moments of revelation upon a mountain top. Moses' comes at Mount Sinai first when God speaks to him 'face to face' in giving the Ten Commandments[128], and then reveals himself to the fullest extent that any human can bear, after Moses has begged forgiveness for his people's sin with the Golden Calf[129].

Elijah's greatest moment of communion with the divine occurs atop Mount Carmel, when he challenges the prophets of the idol Baal to prove the existence of their god. He confronts four hundred and fifty idolatrous prophets and bids them build an altar, place a bull upon it and summon fire from heaven to burn the sacrifice. The heathen priests work themselves up into a frenzy for a whole day, entreating their god, praying, shouting, dancing, cutting themselves. Elijah taunts them 'perhaps your god is asleep, shout louder', Of course nothing happens. Towards the end of the day Elijah builds his own altar, douses it with water, prays to God and sure enough fire falls from heaven and consumes not only the sacrifice but even the stones and soil of the damp altar. Elijah's status is proclaimed as the true prophet of God; the priests of Baal are consigned to oblivion.

Back at the mountain-top meeting, Jesus's face is changed and his clothing altered. But he is not the only person to experience such a bizarre, mystical event. The same thing happens to Moses, following the giving of the Ten Commandments.

So it was that Moses came down from Mount Sinai. And the two tablets of testimony were in Moses's hand as he descended from the mountain. And Moses did not know that the skin of his face had beamed light when God spoke to him ... And when Aaron and all the people of Israel saw Moses, behold, the skin of his face beamed light; and they were afraid to come close to him ... And Moses put a veil upon his face....And whenever Moses went in before the Lord to speak with Him, he would take the veil off until he came out; then he would come out and speak to the children of Israel whatever he had been commanded. And whenever the children of Israel saw the face of Moses, that the skin of Moses's face shone, then Moses would put the veil on his face again, until he went in to speak with Him.[130]

Jesus's clothes and appearance change, like Moses, as a physical manifestation of the change in his status.

Both Moses and Elijah have their spiritual greatness proclaimed atop a mountain. And at the Transfiguration Jesus too is elevated by a heavenly voice declaring him 'my son'. The Transfiguration is the moment that Jesus's spiritual elevation is proclaimed, and even though Moses and Elijah are present this is a private affair with the witnesses sworn to secrecy.

But it is the oddest part of this episode which should interest us the most, for this is where we start to draw the threads together and find the gospels giving us a hint of their concealed agenda. In Luke's words, after Moses and Elijah appear to Jesus, the disciple Peter says:

"Master, it is good for us to be here. Let us put up three shelters — one for you, one for Moses and one for Elijah." He did not know what he was saying[131].

Mark adds that Peter did not know what he was saying because he was so frightened[132]. But even if he was frightened his utterance is puzzling. He and his friends witness their master in communion with the long dead Moses and Elijah- whom they seem to recognise without any difficulty and the only thing he can think of saying is :Let's put up shelters! And one each for that matter. Is this not a bit odd? There must be more here than meets the eye.

The English translations of Matthew's gospel derive from a Greek original. The original no longer exists, but in the Greek versions that have come down to us, the word that we have translated as 'shelters' in Matthew's utterance is σκηνη, pronounced *skay-nay*. This same word occurs in the ancient Greek version of the Jewish Bible[133], to describe the shelters, or tabernacles that the Israelites dwelt in when they came out of Egypt, from which the festival of Tabernacles gets its name. More commonly, the word describes a temporary hut that workers in the field would erect for shelter from the heat during the harvest season[134].

It is also used to refer to shelters that were erected during a ceremony that started in the old Jerusalem Temple, a ceremony described in detail by the Mishnah, the 2nd century compendium of Jewish law, a ceremony that Jesus and his disciples would have witnessed and been familiar with. This ceremony is the strange ritual of the scapegoat, and it is likely that Peter thinks that Moses, Elijah and Jesus are engaged in some sort esoteric rite based on this ceremony.

The Scapegoat

The scapegoat ritual is prescribed in the book of Leviticus, the third of Moses' five books. It is a sacrificial rite that is disturbing to modern sensibilities, not only since it involves the slaughter of an animal, but because of the particularly gruesome way in which the sacrifice was carried out.

Performed by the high priest, it took place on the Day of Atonement, the holiest day of the Jewish calendar. The central rite of this day was the burning of incense by the high priest in the holy of holies, the sacred chamber at the heart of the Temple. The only object in the holy of holies was the golden ark of the covenant; a replica of the original ark, constructed in the wilderness as the Israelites journeyed from Egypt to the promised land which had contained the Ten Commandments, the two tablets of stone that Moses brought down from Mount Sinai. The sanctuary containing the ark was so revered that the high priest was the only mortal permitted to enter therein, and even he was only allowed to do so on this particular day in each year, and then only at prescribed moments, when he would have to be specially clothed in white linen garments.

After concluding the incense ritual in the holy of holies the high priest's assistants would bring him two goats, that had been selected for the occasion. He would stand in front of the goats, with one on either side. Reaching into an urn he would draw two small plaques – originally made of wood, later refashioned in gold, and place one on the head of each goat. On one plaque would be written, 'For the Lord', and on the other 'For Azazel'. The goat designated for the Lord was taken away and offered up on the Temple altar in the regular manner of a sacrifice. The goat designated for Azazel was sent off into the wilderness, bearing the sins of Israel. It falls to its death from a mountain top in the wilderness. Azazel's goat dies for Israel's sins.

According to the biblical account

The goat on which the lot fell for Azazel shall be presented alive before the Lord to make atonement over it, that it may be sent away into the wilderness to Azazel … Aaron shall lay both his hands on the head of the live goat, confess over it all the iniquities of the children of Israel, and all their transgressions, concerning all their sins, he shall place them on the head of the goat, and send it away into the wilderness by the hand of a man made ready. The goat shall bear on itself all their iniquities to an uninhabited land; and he shall release the goat in the wilderness. [135]

Azazel's goat was given a particular English name by William Tyndale, the 16th century biblical translator: he called it a scapegoat. The scapegoat came to symbolise a person or object which was singled out to receive the blame or punishment for the sins of others.

In Christian theology Jesus dies to redeem the sins of those who believed in him. This theme recurs throughout early Christian literature, most clearly in Paul's writings, but is also discernible in the gospels:

For God did not send His son into the world to condemn the world, but that the world through him might be saved. [136]
... the bread that I shall give is my flesh, which I shall give for the life of the world. [137]
... the son of man did not come to be served, but to serve, and to give his life a ransom for many. [138]

Peter knows that Jesus will be a scapegoat and that he will die to redeem the sins of the world. But why should he consider the Transfiguration to be connected with the scapegoat ritual; why does he suggest that he makes booths for Jesus and his interlocutors?

The answer lies in the performance of the scapegoat ritual during Jesus's lifetime and in the discussion that Jesus has with Peter and the other disciples immediately before Moses and Elijah appear. He tells them of his impending death.

From that time on Jesus began to explain to his disciples that he must go to Jerusalem and suffer many things at the hands of the elders, chief priests and teachers of the law, and that he must be killed and on the third day be raised to life. Peter took him aside and began to rebuke him. "Never, Lord!" he said. "This shall never happen to you!" Jesus turned and said to Peter, "Get behind me, Satan! You are a stumbling block to me; you do not have in mind the things of God, but the things of men." [139].

Peter is told that the teacher whom he idolises is to is to die, and in the next breath he is accused by that same teacher of being Satan. In the course of one short conversation his whole world collapses. It is not hard to imagine how shocked, indeed trauma-tised, he feels. And the very next thing to happen is that Jesus takes him up a mountain, where Peter sees him converse with two ancient, dead sages! It is not surprising that Peter thinks this is all a prelude to Jesus's death. Knowing Jesus is to fulfil his mission as a scapegoat and given the location of the event upon a mountain top in the wilderness, he assumes that Moses and Elijah have been designated to lead Jesus to his death. Trying to avoid another rebuke from Jesus, he asks if he should set the event in a ritual context, by making booths which, as we will see, were a prominent feature of the first century scapegoat ritual. Of course he has totally misread the situation, which is why Luke's gospel says that he does not know what he is saying.

His shock at the news that Jesus will die, followed by his bewildering experience at the Transfiguration leads Peter to imagine that Moses and Elijah are about to enact a scapegoat ceremony- conducting Jesus to a gruesome demise in a rocky wasteland.

What Peter fails to recognise in his distress is that Jesus has also told him that he will be resurrected. He seems to be so overwhelmed by the fact of his master's mortality that he overlooks the main point, that Jesus's death is merely to be a transitory demonstration of his *immortality.*

Peter misunderstands the purpose of the Transfiguration and thinks that he is about to witness a scapegoat ceremony. Peter overlooks the fact that Jesus has told him he will be resurrected. These two failings on Peter's part are connected. The Transfiguration and the Resurrection, each of which represent the victory of spirit over matter are both defining moments in understanding the concealed message of the gospels.

We might now understand why Peter is upset, and why he asks the question about booths. But we still don't know what the Transfiguration episode is really about. It is nothing to do with the death of the scapegoat as Peter thought. But if is to establish Jesus as the messiah or the son of God, as the heavenly voice indicates, then what were Moses and Elijah's roles?

The Transfiguration, the most mystically obscure moment in the life of Jesus is also the key to understanding the hidden agenda of the gospels. Even though, as we will see, later gospel editors may have sought to erase or obscure the hidden agenda, they found it too deeply woven within this profound and puzzling narrative to fully excise it. We need to look more closely at the clues contained within the Transfiguration account. And to pay particular attention to the significance of the clothes that turned white.

6

Barabbas the Messianic Pretender

Peter's misreading of the Transfiguration as a scapegoat ceremony was due to his emotional state. Had he not just heard the news that Jesus was to die, he would almost certainly have realised that it would have been impossible for Moses and Elijah to carry out a scapegoat ritual, along the lines of that prescribed in Leviticus, because one of the essential ingredients was missing. Leviticus states quite clearly that there were to be two candidates for the scapegoat, and that the hapless victim was to be chosen by lottery.

The casting out of the goat chosen by lottery is in itself a surviving element of a pagan belief in demons, and the rituals involved in appeasing them. In pagan times the casting out of the goat would have involved human sacrifice. Two people would be brought before the tribe. One would be obliged to slaughter the other and in turn was exiled into the wilderness, in order to drive away sin. The late Hyam Maccoby developed this idea and referred to the exiled participant as the Sacred Executioner. The tribe is protected from the guilt of murder by shifting it onto the Sacred Executioner, who carries it into exile with him, where he is in turn protected by the god of the tribe, or in some versions by the evil god of the wilderness.

Maccoby claims that we see the outlines of such a story in murder myths that occur in a variety of cultures. These include the killing of Abel, Adam and Eve's second son, by his older brother Cain; the death of the Egyptian god of the underworld Osiris, killed by his brother Seth, who trapped him in a chest and threw him into the Nile; and in the ancient Semitic contest between Baal, the chief of the gods and Mot, the god of death who summoned and ultimately prevailed over him. The legend is also the source, according to Maccoby, of the slaughter of Remus by his brother and co-founder of Rome, Romulus; of the murder of the Norse god Balder engineered by the mischievous Loki, and even of the Greek tale of Oedipus and his father. [140]

In each of these myths, one of the pair dies and the other survives. This is also the case in the biblical account, in which the surviving goat was merely let loose in the wilderness. And although Leviticus has taken the sting out of the ritual by replacing human participants with animals, by the time we reach the Temple period, possibly a thousand years after Leviticus, the practice has become more gruesome and the significance of Peter's desire to make booths has become apparent

He bound a thread of crimson wool on the head of the he-goat which was to be sent away, and stood it at the gate from which it was to be sent ... he laid his two hands upon it and he made confession ... They handed the goat over to the man who was to lead it away ... There were ten booths from Jerusalem to the Zok [the place where the goat was taken] ... At every booth they would say to him: here is food and here is water. They went with him from booth to booth, except the last one. For they would not go with him up to the Zok, but they would stand from afar, and watch what he was doing ... He divided the thread of crimson wool, and tied one half to the rock, the other half between its horns, and pushed it from behind. And it went rolling down and before it had reached half its way down hill it was dashed to pieces. [141]

In this account, which was written about a century after the Jerusalem Temple was destroyed and the last goat had been dispatched into the wilderness, a new factor is introduced. Unlike the biblical account the goat is not just sent into the wilderness. It is pushed over a cliff – the Zok seems to be a high mountain ledge – and killed; cut to pieces on the rocks below. The goat that carries sins, dies. Maccoby suggests that this is to avoid the possibility that the goat, having been allowed to wander into the wilderness, strays back into the town bringing the sins with it.

Peter, in considering that Jesus was to be led into the wilderness by Moses and Elijah, has failed to spot that there was no lottery. Jesus, at the time of the Transfiguration, could not have been destined to die the death of a scapegoat, because he had not been selected from a pair of candidates; the essential ingredient of chosenness was missing.

Not so, however at the crucifixion. When we look in detail at Jesus's death on the cross we will see parallels with many elements of the scapegoat ritual. Peter was right that Jesus would be a scapegoat and that there would be a ceremony at which he would be slaughtered to expiate sin. It is just that Peter got the timing and location wrong.

The Crucifixion

A lottery did indeed take place at the crucifixion. In fact, there were two lotteries, and both are recorded in each of the four gospels. In one event the gospels clearly indicate that lots were drawn, in the other event the element of ballot is merely alluded to.

Jesus's crucifixion seems not to have been a foregone conclusion. Even at a very late stage the crowd had the opportunity to save his life:

> And at that time they had a notorious prisoner called Barabbas. Therefore, when they had gathered together, Pilate said to them, 'Whom do you want me to release to you? Barabbas, or Jesus who is called Christ?' ... They said, 'Barabbas!' Pilate said to them, 'What then shall I do with Jesus who is called Christ?' They all said to him, 'Let him be crucified!' Then the governor said, 'Why, what evil has he done?' But they cried out all the more, saying, 'Let him be

crucified!' When Pilate saw that he could not prevail at all, but rather that a tumult was rising, he took water and washed his hands before the multitude, saying, 'I am innocent of the blood of this just person. You see to it.' And all the people answered and said, 'his blood be on us and on our children.'[142]

Pilate's washing his hands of the affair is a literary allusion to the ceremony prescribed in Deuteronomy should a murdered corpse be found in the fields, and it is not known who the murderer was. In that case the elders of the nearest city sacrifice a calf, wash their hands over it and say 'our hands did not slaughter this blood and our eyes did not see it'. [143] It is unlikely that Pilate who, unlike the *matronas*, was not known for his interest in Israelite culture really said this. Once again it is an example of the gospels establishing a literary connection with the Jewish Bible.

And they all cried out at once, saying, 'Away with this man, and release to us Barabbas'— who had been thrown into prison for a certain rebellion made in the city, and for murder. Pilate, therefore, wishing to release Jesus, again called out to them. But they shouted, saying, 'Crucify him, crucify him!' Then he said to them the third time, 'Why, what evil has he done? I have found no reason for death in him. I will therefore chastise him and let him go.' But they were insistent, demanding with loud voices that he be crucified. And the voices of these men and of the chief priests prevailed. So Pilate gave sentence that it should be as they requested. And he released to them the one they requested, who for rebellion and murder had been thrown into prison; but he delivered Jesus to their will. [144]

During his lifetime Jesus was one of many itinerant preachers, prophets of hope or doom in a subjugated and unhappy Roman province. His active supporters would have adored him, and those who were not his followers would most likely have followed popular opinion in their enthusiasm, or lack of it, for him. It is hard to conceive of a mob which was so passionately opposed to him that they would bellow for his death at the hand of the Roman oppressor. Furthermore, since Judaism takes vows very seriously, the idea that the crowd would have held their children responsible for his death is preposterous. The passage from Matthew has long been seen as a polemic against the Jews for the church's own theological reasons.

But if the crowd did not say what Matthew accounts, then what it was about Barabbas that made the crowd seek his freedom?

Although Luke, and also Mark, describe Barabbas as guilty of rebellion and murder, the other gospels are less forthright. Matthew calls him a 'notorious prisoner' and John calls him a 'robber'. So what exactly was he? Why the reluctance to detail his offence?

If, as Luke states in the above passage Barabbas had been condemned for *a certain rebellion made in the city* then it is understandable why the crowd would want him released. The Roman occupation was deeply unpopular and the Jews were in constant revolt against their oppressors. Josephus considers Judea to be the most troublesome province in the whole history of the Roman empire. One can imagine that Barabbas, by participating in, or leading a 'certain rebellion' would be a popular hero. Yet gospel accounts suggest that the crowd are less interested in Barabbas's release than Jesus's crucifixion. And only a week earlier Jesus had made a triumphant, popularly acclaimed entrance into Jerusalem.[145] Why would the crowd now abandon him so whimsically? This question becomes even more baffling if we consider Matthew's account of the same incident and the words that he places into the mouths of the mob: 'His blood be upon us and upon our children'. This is an extreme, lengthy, and unnecessary slogan to put into the mouths of a mob, particularly one that had so enthusiastically welcomed him as he entered Jerusalem on his donkey the previous Sunday.

But what if Barabbas was not simply a bandit but a prominent member of a band of revolutionaries against the Roman state. We saw earlier that those who led revolts against Rome were often considered to be the messiah, the example of Bar Kochba, or Bar Koziba, being the best known. If Barabbas was a revolutionary fighter he, like Jesus, could be a claimant to the title of messiah. What if Pilate had two messianic candidates before him? One, a spiritual leader, Jesus, whom his followers considered to conform to Isaiah's messianic ideal – a man who would restore peace and harmony to the world; and the other, Barabbas, a messiah in Ezekiel's model of a military leader who would restore political independence to Israel. The crucifixion seems to have taken place at Passover. It would not be unthinkable for the Romans to have designated the Passover festival, the season in which Israel celebrated its redemption from Egypt, the time of year when the future Jewish redemption was expected to take place, as an appropriate time to execute messianic candidates.

If this seems a little speculative, consider Barabbas's name. Although the name is found in the later Babylonian-Jewish literature of the 4-6th centuries, it is unattested in Jewish sources of the period we are discussing. Barabbas is a Greek form of the Aramaic name Bar Abba, which means son of the father. A strange name. Unless we write it in capitals. Son of the Father. An epithet that also described Jesus:

Lord Jesus Christ, the son of the father[146]
God has sent forth the spirit of his son into your hearts, crying out, 'Abba, Father!'[147]
'I will be to him a Father, and he shall be to me a son'[148]

Is the name 'Son of the Father an indication of messianic aspirations? Could Barabbas have been a messianic pretender, with Pilate asking the crowd which Messiah they wanted to save? Was Jesus condemned to death by chance, a lottery in which the decision of the mob replaced the lots drawn from a box? Jesus the scapegoat, dying to atone for Israel, chosen by lottery in Jerusalem, in a Roman mockery of the High Priest's ritual.

The Christian Bible makes no further mention of Barabbas. His life was saved by Jesus's death. The voice of the crowd was the ballot that both saved and exiled him. He becomes the elusive wanderer exiled into history, the Sacred Executioner who carries the sins of the tribe into the wilderness, effecting atonement for the people. Barabbas the scapegoat, chosen by lottery.

This would all be very neat, had Barabbas performed the role of scapegoat, exiled into the wilderness to carry the people's sins away. But this was not his role. He did not carry the sins of the people into the wilderness. It was Jesus's death that effected atonement, not Barabbas' exile, if indeed he was ever exiled. The Barabbas narrative introduces the idea of lottery into the crucifixion drama. But in the form in which it has been transmitted to us, it does not fit into the scapegoat model. It may serve some other theological purpose, or it may be that the received story is incomplete, corrupted over time as is so often the case with ancient texts.

Furthermore, the lottery that selected Jesus as the sacrificial victim was conducted by the crowd, not by the executioner. Whereas the slaughtered goat in the ancient Temple ritual was elected in a ballot drawn by the priest, the man who would himself butcher one goat and exile the other. The crucifixion lottery should have been conducted by Pilate himself, playing the role of the priest, the goat's executioner. It should not have been left to the will of the congregation assembled in the Temple. Yet it was precisely the congregation, the roar of the mob, that chose Jesus over Barabbas. Something is missing from the selection of Barabbas. Lots were not drawn, the decisive vote was the will of the people.

And so we must turn to the second lottery in the crucifixion narrative. One conducted by the sacrificers themselves, the 'priests' in the twisted sacrificial rite. The Roman soldiers.

The lottery of the clothes

The narrative of the crucifixion is one of the most well known episodes in human history. Even discounting for a moment its religious significance, it has emerged as perhaps the single most powerful cultural icon in the Western world. It is the subject of countless artistic masterpieces, has been reworked time and again in prose and poetry, and inspired dozens of the world's finest composers. The story, in broad outline, is as familiar to us as any national myth or folk tale, with the result that a primitive and barbaric form of execution has become a byword in every language under the sun.

And yet there is one element of the crucifixion account which is relatively unknown to those who do not actively profess the Christian faith. Its obscurity is odd because it is mentioned in every gospel. It is therefore far better documented in the original sources than, for example, the stations of the cross or the immaculate conception, both of which are later additions to Christianity. It has probably been overlooked simply because it seems to be a parenthetic irrelevance, inserted into the narrative for no apparent reason. But it is quite possibly the most important part of the narrative, the key to a true understanding of the significance of the crucifixion.

This underrated episode occurs in each of the four gospels, but the account in John is far more expansive. The synoptic gospels, as is their wont, are broadly similar in their presentation:

Then they crucified him, and divided his garments, casting lots, that it might be fulfilled that which was spoken by the prophet: 'They divided my garments among them, and for my clothing they cast lots.'[149]

And when they crucified him, they divided his garments, casting lots for them to determine what every man should take. [150]

And when they had come to the place called Calvary, there they crucified him, and the criminals, one on the right hand and the other on the left. Then Jesus said, "Father, forgive them, for they do not know what they do." And they divided his garments and cast lots. [151]

But John provides a level of detail and explanation far surpassing this:

Then the soldiers, when they had crucified Jesus, took his garments and made four parts, to each soldier a part, and also the tunic. Now the tunic was without seam, woven from the top in one piece. They said therefore among themselves, "Let us not tear it, but cast lots for it, whose it shall be," that the scripture might be fulfilled which says: "They divided my garments among them, and for my clothing they cast lots." Therefore the soldiers did these things. [152]

In Matthew, Mark, and Luke lots were cast for all Jesus's garments. Not so in the gospel of John, Here, one of the garments, the tunic, seems to be of particular significance. The other garments were divided and shared out, but only the tunic, which itself was apparently of a peculiar, noteworthy construction was subjected to a lottery.

The second lottery in the crucifixion narrative is more clearly identified by the gospel writers than that in which Barabbas was chosen. The Roman soldiers cast lots amongst themselves to determine which of Jesus's garments they will each take. We don't know why this is, although both Matthew and John inform us that the act of distributing Jesus's clothes by lot was necessary in order to comply with Psalm 22. But unless we know the significance of Psalm 22, that doesn't really help us.

Psalm 22

Psalm 22 is considered by Christian theologians to be one of the passages from the Jewish Bible which predict Jesus as messiah, and foretell his crucifixion and redemption. It opens with the words 'My God, my God, why have You forsaken me?' Jesus proclaims these very words, but translated into his native Aramaic tongue, on the cross:

Eli, Eli, lama sabachthani. [153]

This utterance is problematic. Are we to believe that Jesus is given to biblical citation in times of extreme crisis so that at the moment of his impending death he can find nothing more anguished to utter than a quotation from the Psalms, however appropriate? Or did a biblical author put these words into his mouth since Psalm 22 was assumed to foretell the crucifixion in much the same way as the book of Isaiah is understood by Christian theologians to contain prophecies about the coming of the Messiah?

As Geza Vermes remarks[154], this utterance was unlikely to have been a deliberate quote from the Psalms. Firstly, the onlookers do not seem to have understood it as a biblical quote, but as a cry for help, an entreaty to the Prophet Elijah, whom Jesus had met at the Transfiguration, Eli being a shortened version of his name: 'Eli, Eli why have your forsaken me?'

Some of those who stood there, when they heard that, said, "This man is calling for Elijah!" [155]

According to Jewish tradition, following his ascent to heaven, Elijah became immortal and wanders the earth in the guise of an old man, performing miracles. Jesus may either be calling for Elijah to rescue him, as part of his regular miracle-working, or he may be alluding to something that transpired at the

Transfiguration – possibly a commitment by Elijah to Jesus, which the latter feels has not been honoured. More importantly, although Vermes seems to discount this, the onlookers at the crucifixion may have linked his cry to the tradition that Elijah will herald the coming of the messiah. They may have assumed that Jesus was castigating Elijah for not having come to proclaim him as messiah, forsaking him and leaving him to his death.

Vermes's second point is that Jesus's cry was in Aramaic, whereas the psalm was written in Hebrew. He argues that worshippers knew the Hebrew psalms by heart, so why then quote them in translation?

There is another question about Jesus's words which relate to the supposed Aramaic word *sabachthani*. In fact no such word exists. The Aramaic for 'have you forsaken me?' is *shavakthani*. It is possible that in fact Jesus was not speaking in Aramaic at all, but in Hebrew: *'eli, eli, lama zavachtani'* 'My, God, my God, why have you <u>sacrificed</u> me?'

Many of the psalms are introduced by a short label identifying the supposed author, or the occasion on which the ode would be recited. Frequently these take the form 'A psalm of David' or 'A psalm for the ascent.' Psalm 22 however has an obscure identifier, of uncertain meaning but often rendered as 'For the musician (or 'singer') upon the morning star (or 'morning gazelle', or 'at the rise of morning').' The ancient Aramaic translation, which Jesus is alleged to have quoted when he cries *eli, eli, lama sabachthani* renders the introduction: 'For the singer, concerning the power of the daily morning sacrifice'. The psalm in its Aramaic translation is therefore identified with the sacrificial Temple ritual.

Whether Jesus cried out 'My God, why have you sacrificed me' or 'My God why have you forsaken me' the effect on those to whom his words were reported would have been the same. In the first case they would have thought of Psalm 22 because it was associated with the daily sacrifice. In the second they would also have thought of this psalm because it would have been assumed he was quoting from it.

Psalm 22 speaks in general terms about a man who is being persecuted by his enemies and who turns to God for salvation. In many translations it contains a resonant phrase, 'they have pierced my hands and feet' which can easily be applied to Jesus on the cross.

This phrase which occurs in many translations of the Bible is inaccurate. It suits the use of this psalm as a prophecy about the crucifixion, but in the original language it does not make grammatical or contextual sense. The Hebrew in Jewish tradition reads, 'dogs have surrounded me, like a lion at my hands and feet'. The Greek translation of the Jewish Bible predates Jesus by about a century. It is often a truer textual witness than the ancient Hebrew manuscripts and confirms the reading 'they have pierced...'. But there is no way of knowing whether this was amended by later editors following the rise of Christianity.

Be not far from me, for trouble is near and there is no-one to help. Many bulls have surrounded me; the mighty ones of Bashan have encircled me. They open their mouths at me, a devouring and roaring lion. I am poured out like water, and all my bones have become separated; my heart is like wax, molten within me. My strength is as dry as pottery, my tongue has been welded to my jaws and you have brought me to the dust of death. For dogs have surrounded me, the congregation of the wicked has encompassed me; they pierced my hands and my feet[156]; I can count all my bones. They look and stare at me. They divide my clothes among them, and over my garment[157] they cast a lottery. [158]

One can see why this psalm was considered to be a description of someone suffering on the cross, and indeed the psalm becomes strongly identified in Christian tradition with the crucifixion. In a wide ranging study, Mark Hoffman tried to discover the significance of the references to Psalm 22 in the Christian Bible, given that there was no evidence that it had been interpreted in a messianic sense prior to Christianity. He considered all the textual variants of the psalm and the way in which it had been interpreted in ancient Jewish and Semitic traditions. He produced a convincing explanation of how and why Psalm 22 *could* be read as a messianic text, portending to the crucifixion, but he could not, upon his own admission show why it *should* be read so.

> *I have explained how Psalm 22 could be helpful in clarifying or supporting a messianic reading, but I have not demonstrated why someone should turn to it rather than to some other Scripture. To put it yet another way, an ancient reader of the Hebrew Bible would not likely choose descriptions of suffering from Psalm 22 to demonstrate that the speaker was a distinguished and unique character. But if that reader were directed to search in Psalm 22 for some distinctive characteristics which could pertain to the psalm's subject, it would be possible according to the rules of ancient Biblical exegesis[159] to find them. [160]*

Hoffman concludes that the psalm became associated with the crucifixion either because Jesus quoted its opening line in Aramaic, *eli, eli, lama sabachthani* , or because somebody thought they heard him say these words. But there is another possibility.

Most of Psalm 22 is written in descriptive terms, the poet describing his suffering and his bodily pain. There are only two specific incidents recounted in it. One is the piercing of his hands and feet, which as we have seen is not supported by the Hebrew text. The other is the dividing of his clothes. If the lottery over Jesus's clothes was of especial theological significance, such that it was described in all four gospels, we can understand why both Matthew and John drew their readers' attention to Psalm 22, which describes a suffering martyr and contains the only biblical allusion to such an incident. Jesus's impulsive and quite under-standable cry 'My God, My God why have you sacrificed me' was mis-rendered as 'why have you forsaken me', possibly as a stylistic device, to put us in mind of the psalm and to lead us to think of the division of garments to which it refers in reality. Psalm 22 becomes important then, not because Jesus was thought to have quoted from it, but because it provides a biblical prophecy concerning the lottery over the clothes.

Despite every gospel recording the lottery over the garments, John makes more of the issue of it than the others. For him one garment, the tunic, stands out as having been allocated by lot. Jesus's other garments were simply shared out amongst the soldiers. Perhaps John is making an exegetical point, drawing our attention to the two words translated respectively as clothes and garments in the Hebrew text, even though there is nothing signif-icant about this sort of repetition. It is just an example of a literary technique which occurs frequently in the psalms, known as parallelism. For purely stylistic reasons a verse expresses the same idea twice in different words; it makes for better poetry, and stresses the point. But there is also a interpretative tradition which argues that every word in the Bible is sacred and has its own particular meaning. Although this was generally limited to the Pentateuch, the Five Books of Moses,, it is possible that the author of John also considered each word in Psalm 22 to be significant and wished to draw the distinction between the two types of clothing to his readers' attention; especially since one word was in the plural, and the other in the singular.

They divide my clothes[161] among them, and over my garment[162] they cast a lottery

John may have had particular reasons for wishing to tell his readers about two specific types of clothing. And in particular, about the nature of the tunic which had to be divided by lot.

John's account differs significantly from all the others; it is the only account to restrict the casting of lots to just one garment, the tunic, which he describes in detail. The soldiers decide not to tear it, implying that it was valuable, possibly of a higher quality than the rags which most convicted criminals wore. But the emphasis in John on this particular garment allows the lottery to fit more closely with Psalm 22,18 which refers to two different type of clothes:

Much has been written about the sequence of events before the crucifixion, in particular the point at which Jesus's clothes were removed, and whether or not they were returned to him to wear on the cross. For our purposes all that matters is that, according to the gospels, Jesus was not taken to his tomb in his clothes. At some point they were removed and he was placed in a shroud. The clothes therefore were discarded and it is conceivable that the soldiers did share them out. After all, what else would happen to the personal possessions of an executed prisoner in those violent times? In any event there seems no reason to doubt the assertion in all four gospels that a lottery took place to apportion Jesus's clothes.

John 19:23

John's gospel shows signs of having been influenced by both Wisdom literature and by Gnosticism.

As we have seen, Wisdom literature is not specifically Jewish. It seems to have emerged in the ancient near east, especially in Egypt and Mesopotamia. As trade and cultures spread and cross-fertilised throughout the near east, Wisdom literature extended its appeal. One branch found its way into Jewish thought, crystallising in biblical books such as Proverbs and Ecclesiastes, the apocryphal Ben Sira and in the Wisdom of Solomon, amongst others. Wisdom was an important motif and concept in Jewish philosophical writings in the centuries before Jesus.

Gnosticism was a complex series of doctrines which took on

various forms. Just as there are many schools of philosophy, so there were many Gnostic systems. In its most basic form it placed its emphasis on the spirit over the body, and sought metaphysical solutions to the questions of existence.

John's book opens by identifying the Word, or Logos, which symbolises higher truth, an idea which recurs in both Gnostic and Wisdom thought. As a consequence of this metaphysical approach, John is more prone than the others to the use of metaphor to illustrate spiritual ideas.

Then the soldiers, when they had crucified Jesus, took his garments and made four parts, to each soldier a part, and also the tunic. Now the tunic was without seam, woven from the top in one piece.

This translation from the standard Greek text of John is taken from the New King James version; but there is more than one way of rendering the verse in English. The New American Standard version translates the final clause in verse 23 as *woven in one piece*. The words *from the top* have disappeared, and are also absent in several other translations.

The Greek text is:

εςκ τω⁺ν ανωθεν υϕϕαντοῦ διϛ οϛλου.

Its literal translation it is:

woven from the upper part through the whole.

However, literal translations are slippery things. Any translator will tell you that when faced with more than one possible ways of translating a word, they have to use their judgement as to what fits the context best. So the translation becomes something of a personal opinion, open to multiple interpretations and never wholly accurate.

The word ανωθεν, pronounced an-o-then, is translated in the King James version as top. The Greek word occurs twelve other times in the Christian Bible. On three occasions it is translated as top. On five occasions the King James translators render it as 'from above' in the sense of 'from heaven', and once as 'from the beginning', in the sense of 'from the beginning of time'. Of the five occasions when an-o-then is translated in the sense of 'from heaven', two occur in John[163] and the remainder occur in James.

What if we were to substitute the translation 'from above' into the verse we are discussing, in place of 'from the top', without changing any of the other words but rearranging the order to fit better with the Greek version? We get:

Now the tunic was without seam, from above, woven in one piece.

And if we understand from above as meaning from heaven, the sense of the clause becomes.

Now the tunic was from heaven, without seam, woven in one piece.

The word which is translated as seamless, or without seam comes from the Greek αραφοß which can also be translated as 'not sewn', or 'unstitched'. In the Aramaic Peshitta version of John – which is regarded by the Eastern Church as more authentic than the Greek text, the garment is described as ܪܠܐ ܪܠܝܐ meaning 'without thread' or possibly 'without stitch'.

In ancient times weavers' looms were small affairs and garments would be made of several pieces of cloth sewn together. A seamless garment would have been rare since it would need to have been made on an unusually large loom. But the meaning of this word may not be that the garment had no seam, rather that it had no border, or hem, or any other sort of stitching upon it. It is probably best therefore to refer to it as an unstitched tunic or robe.

And quite improbably the unstitched robe, as we shall call it brings us unexpectedly to one of the great mysteries and romances of western folklore. The mystery of the holy grail.

7

The Holy Grail

The legend of the Holy Grail has captured the imagination of millions of people for hundreds of years. It contains all the elements of successful literature – adventure, religion, violence and romance. Those who quest for it are heroes of a more innocent age. When we read the English grail classics, including Thomas Malory's *Morte d'Arthur* and T. H. White's *Once and Future King* we are transported to a chivalrous world, in which good can be clearly differentiated from bad, and courtly heroes will rescue us from dragons. The lost grail represents the only element of uncertainty in this uncomplicated universe. This gives it an almost subversive quality, as it hints at a more complex reality, one which threatens to impinge upon the comfort of fantasy. The grail's most enduring feature is its sheer mystery; the quest for an unknown, for something whose identity will not be revealed until it is discovered.

Although it is said to be a sacred Christian relic the grail has become associated with the King Arthur saga, a genre that straddles the boundary between Christianity and Dark Age paganism. The Christian Knights of the Round Table seek the grail under the protective influence of the Celtic priestess Morgan le Fay and the Druid prophet cum magician Merlin. As such the grail holds far greater significance for new-age apostles, pagans, and conspiracy theorists than it does for mainstream theologians and clerics. A Google search returns twice as many results for 'Holy Grail' than for 'Virgin Mary'. A Holy Grail has become a synonym for a much sought after but unattainable goal; it has entered management speech and the political vocabulary.

The unknown nature of the Holy Grail sets it apart from other religious items. The medieval church claimed to have identified thousands of relics, objects pertaining to Jesus, his disciples, and later saints. Yet none of these tangible objects, however spurious their attribution has attracted anything like as much attention, and has been the focus of so much intellectual activity, as the grail. Should the Turin Shroud, alleged to be the garment in which Jesus's body was wrapped, ever be conclusively proved as authentic it will, despite its historical and religious significance, immediately lose its appeal to conspiracy theorists; in much the same way as the Garden of Gethsemane which is likely to be the site of the Last Supper holds little interest for the curious and the lover of adventure. The grail legends are fed by human curiosity; it is the mystery surrounding the object that has proved to be its most enduring quality. Of course, there are many lost religious items deserving of a quest, just waiting to have a good adventure story written about their discovery. One of the best known is the lost Ark of the Covenant, which vanished two and a half millennia ago, but nevertheless made it onto our cinema screens in the late twentieth century. Yet while Stephen Spielberg's film Raiders of the Lost Ark may have been a Hollywood smash, it is hard to see how any treatment of the subject could engage the public imagination in the same way as contemporary books such as The Da Vinci Code or the earlier Holy Blood and Holy Grail have done for the grail.

Why? Because from the outset the audience knew, or if they did not know, were soon apprised of the fact, that the lost Ark was a fabulous golden chest, constructed by the Israelites during their wanderings through the wilderness. It originally contained the Ten Commandments that Moses brought down from Mount Sinai, and was housed in the Holy of Holies, the very place that the Jewish high priest entered just once a year to effect atonement for his people. When Nebuchadnezzar, king of Babylon sacked Jerusalem in 580 BCE the Ark was taken from Solomon's Temple and was never seen again. So although a quest for the lost Ark, protected by all sorts of magical and demonic powers provides the foundation for a good yarn, the thousand year history of Holy Grail legends has included an additional, beguiling element of mystery. Nobody knows what it is. Its seekers are not at all sure what they are looking for. They seek it, confident only in the knowledge that they will know it when they find it.

The quest for the Holy Grail is therefore not just an adventure story, nor a search for a lost religious icon. It is a pursuit for truth, a mission to uncover a hidden reality. In many ways it is a spiritual quest in itself, a search for a concealed dimension, a revelation in the making. It does not rely on the seeker having supernatural qualities, as did the great questers of Greek mythology such as Jason or Perseus. Anyone can search for the grail. In medieval times all they needed was knightly companions, today internet access and a good imagination will suffice. This is why the grail has spawned such a vast literature, is the subject of so many websites, why it has become an object of veneration in itself, irrespective of what it may be. It has inspired works as diverse as Wagner's *Parsifal*, Umberto Eco's *Foucaults' Pendulum* and even Monty Python.

The first written account that we have concerning the grail was composed by Chretien de Troyes, a raconteur in late 12th century France. His tale, Perceval ou Le Conte du Graal, is an Arthurian romance, about a young knight of the Round Table, Percival, and his discovery of the grail in the castle of the Fisher King.

Contrary to popular belief de Troyes does not tell us what he thinks the Holy Grail is. That is left to later writers. Two principal legends emerge. One, that it was a chalice, a cup into which Jesus's blood had been poured at the crucifixion. The other was that it was the cup that Jesus used at the Last Supper, which had been brought to England shortly after the crucifixion by Joseph of Arimathea. Whatever its function, all agreed that it was a cup. Its symbolic character therefore was linked to the holy communion, the church rite in which the body and blood of Jesus are represented by a wafer and a chalice of wine.

But modern scholars have challenged the view of the grail as a cup. Theories range from conventional associations with the Eucharist, in which the grail becomes the holy blood itself to modern theorists such as Jessie Weston, for whom it represented pagan fertility rites, or Joseph Campbell, who saw it as symbolising an inner spiritual or psychological quest.

The debate over the grail's identity comes down to one question. Was there a holy chalice, known as a 'graal' in the tongue of the medieval French story tellers, which was somehow connected with the betrayal and crucifixion of Jesus, and which disappeared following Jesus's death on the cross to become the stuff of legend? Or did the medieval bards build on an existing legend about an obscure and unidentifiable sacred 'graal', and, being French speakers, naturally assume it referred to a cup?

Current scholarship (and we have to use that word loosely since much of what has been written on the subject is fantastic and speculative) assumes that the legend of the grail existed long before de Troyes. The earliest legends are likely to have been transmitted orally, circulating in learned circles in the monasteries and delivered to the public in preachers' homilies and by wandering troubadours. It first reached a mass audience in the Arthurian legends, most notably in Malory's Morte d'Arthur where it came to symbolise an object of purity and perfection, which could only be discovered by someone pure of heart and perfect of body, as epitomised by Sir Gawain. The quest for the grail became a personal search for sanctity and unspoiled virtue.

In The Holy Blood and Holy Grail, first published in 1982, Henry Lincoln, Michael Baigent, and Richard Leigh put forward a different theory. They tried to show that the French expression, sangraal or sangreal, which is understood to mean Holy Grail, had long been misunderstood. It was not a corruption of sante graal but of sang real, meaning royal blood. The true Holy Grail was not a chalice, but an allusion to the royal blood line, the lineage of the Hebrew King David. David's lineage continued in a direct line through Jesus, to his descendants. It was no longer the royal house of Israel but the messianic dynasty.

The keepers of the mystery of the Holy Grail, according to this theory, were the custodians of the secret of Jesus's unpublicised marriage to Mary Magdalene. The couple had a son, or possibly several children. Following the crucifixion, the family fled to south-west France and their descendants engendered the ancient Merovingian royal dynasty who ruled northern and eastern France, and western Germany between the 5th and 7th centuries. These guardians of the grail were the Knights Templar who had discovered proof of Jesus's marriage in Jerusalem. They deposited the evidence, whatever it was, with the Cathars, a mysterious sect of knights and mystics, who lived in the Languedoc region of France. The Cathars themselves were persecuted and ultimately destroyed by the Roman church in the 13th century, in what seems to be the only crusade conducted by the church against Christians, apparently in order to suppress the secret that they preserved. For, according to the book's authors, had word got out that Jesus had married and sired children the entire Christian faith would have been undermined.

Would a faith which had grown to dominate the Western world fail to withstand the disclosure of an historical fact, had it been true? It may have caused a few problems for the proponents of celibacy amongst the Catholic priesthood, but that is happening anyway. There is nothing in Christianity which ultimately would have been negated or threatened had Jesus produced children.

Much evidence has been adduced both in support of the theory of Jesus's blood line, and against it. The balance of probability lies with the sceptics. The idea that the mystery of the Holy Grail is connected with a royal dynasty founded by Jesus's descendants, and that in some vaguely defined way this conceals a deeper mystery connected with female deity worship, as suggested in some texts, just does not hold water.

The trouble with all grail theories, even the most rigorously argued, is that they are predicated on folklore. They begin with the assumption that there was such a thing as the Holy Grail and seek to prove what it was, but the only evidence that they have for its existence is a literary tradition. This is like trying to prove who Cinderella's grandmother was. It doesn't matter how much evidence one tries to bring, for unless we know who Cinderella was, we cannot identify her grandmother. We can write a great story about her, but all we are doing is creating one piece of folklore from another, constructing facts out of fantasy.

If we believe that there was such a thing as the Holy Grail, we can only investigate it rigorously using scientific techniques. For example, if we were trying to prove that Francis Bacon wrote a play that was historically attributed to Shakespeare, we would look for correspondences and contrasts between the work under question and other works by both Bacon and Shakespeare. Should we want to show that a painting of Venice was by Canaletto himself and not one of his school we would compare details from known masterpieces by the master, including brushwork and palette. Similarly if we want to prove the existence of the Holy Grail – which is the essential first step in identifying it – we have to look for it in context. Where would we expect to find it and can we construct a hypothesis that we can test, using other known facts?

As far as Bible studies goes, this need to establish the veracity of a fact before trying to explain it does not just apply to the Holy Grail. The same argument can be applied to those who wish to challenge, or prove, key biblical episodes, such as Mary's virginity, and Moses's revelation at Sinai. We have to ask how Jesus could be descended through the paternal line from King David if his mother was a virgin; and we have to be able to prove

Moses's existence before we can discuss his experiences at Mount Sinai. So if we believe the Holy Grail exists, we have to start by looking at what the Bible has to say. We cannot assume, as all grail theorists have done up to now, that the Bible is silent about it.

For it is most certainly not silent about the Holy Grail, a real object that is attested in all four gospels. It was connected with Jesus's crucifixion and for his followers it had a sacred character. But it was not a cup, it was an article of clothing. Its source lies in the book of Leviticus and is expanded upon in a Psalm of the Jewish Bible. We can identify it using the midrashic technique of cross-referencing language and context between biblical passages. It is the article of clothing we have been discussing. It is the unstitched robe.

The main language spoken in Israel during the period when Jesus and his followers lived was Aramaic, part of the Semitic family of languages, which also includes Hebrew and Arabic. Hebrew was not the day-to-day language of the Jews, but was the scholarly language of religion and literature. It played a role similar to that of Latin in England from medieval times to the nineteenth century –it was not used in day to day speech but educated people knew and understood it. It played a formal role in legal documentation and religion. The Jewish Bible had been written almost exclusively in Hebrew, at a time when it was still the vernacular, although Aramaic words occur in many books, and some of the later ones, particularly that of Daniel, contain substantial portions of Aramaic. The Christian Bible may have first been transmitted orally in Aramaic, although scholars believe that the earliest written versions were in Greek.

Aramaic and Hebrew, in common with all Semitic languages are based on consonantal roots. This means that different parts of speech for the same word share the same consonants, whilst the vowels change. Think of the English infinitive *to fight*. The past participle is *fought*, containing the same consonants but with different vowels. We find the same, for example, with *raise* and *rose*, or *speak* and *spoke*. The vowels change, but the consonants remain identical. These forms, exceptions in the English language, are the norm in Semitic languages. If the examples we have used were Semitic words we would say that their roots are *fght*, *rs*, and *spk* respectively; the constant consonants are known as the root of the word, whilst the vowels vary according to tense, number, and person.

In fact vowels are not considered as part of the Semitic alphabets, which are comprised solely of consonants. The vowels are there simply to assist pronunciation and may be indicated in a written text by marks above or below the line, although in most texts designed for native speakers they are not indicated at all. In the majority of Hebrew and Aramaic words the roots consist of just three consonants.

When the Israelites go out into the desert in the early morning and discover that a miraculous food is lying on the ground waiting to be gathered they ask, 'What is it?' The archaic Hebrew word used to mean 'what' is *mn*. When the word enters the English vocabulary we get *Manna*. Same consonants, new vowels.

God creates the world in six days and rests on the seventh. The Hebrew word meaning to rest is *sh-b-t*. In English it has come down to us as Sabbath.

When Leviticus tells us that the high priest stood in front of the two goats and drew lots from an urn, the word it uses for a 'lot' is *goral*. Strip away the vowels and we get the consonantal root *grl*. The same root exists in Arabic to mean stony ground or pebbles. *Goral* probably acquired its meaning as a 'lot' because in ancient times distinctive pebbles may have been used as the lots in a lottery.

Does the root *grl* look familiar? It should do, because if *grail* were a Hebrew word its root would also be *grl* – the same root as the Hebrew word for a 'lot'. The word *grail* is simply a transliteration of the Hebrew roof *grl* and the Christian Bible is full of similar transliterations from Hebrew and Aramaic. Most of them are names or technical terms which were imported into the original gospels, that had been written in Greek. They were imported as they stood rather than translated because there was no direct Greek equivalent. From there they were transmitted in a similar transliterated form into the modern translations. Well known examples of this are the Aramaic phrases that Jesus is quoted as using, *talitha kumi,* [164] meaning 'young girl, arise' and *eli, eli, lama sabachthani*[165] which as we have argued means 'My God, My God why have you sacrificed me'. But there are other transliterated words in the New Testament which we just take for granted, scarcely aware of their Semitic origin. These include the word amen, rabbi, satan, mammon. Grail is just another of these words, even though it does not appear in the gospels, a Hebrew root the vowels of which shifted slightly as they were transmitted orally by storytellers.

The word grail then is a corruption of *goral*. The Holy Grail did not derive from the old French word for a chalice as the medieval story tellers imagined. It was called a *goral* or *grl* or *grail* long before the legend reached twelfth century France. The Holy Grail was certainly not a misinterpretation of the words *sang real* meaning holy blood, referring to the mythical descendants of Jesus and Mary Magdalene. It was not a cup or chalice. The Holy Grail means the holy lot. It refers to the unstitched garments over which the soldiers drew lots.

The Grail at the Crucifixion

So the Holy Grail, this mysterious stuff of fact and legend turns out to be the unstitched robe, divided by Roman soldiers at the crucifixion. But why? What is there about the idea of this garment, or of garments in general, which would have necessitated the introduction of the unstitched robe into the crucifixion narrative?

Garments played a surprisingly important role in the

philosophy of early Christian sects.

In its earliest days various expressions of Christianity evolved with differing and complex theologies. Amongst them was a form which has become known as the Syriac tradition, originating as the name suggests in Syria and the north-eastern parts of Israel. The religious texts that belong to this tradition are rich in metaphor, and make extensive use of clothing as a means of describing the spiritual nature of their subjects.

One of the most important articles of faith for Syriac Christianity was the belief in the renewal of the world that existed before Adam and Eve were exiled from the Garden of Eden. Genesis recounts that God made clothes for Adam[166] and according to the Syriac tradition, Adam's garments of glory were reclaimed by Jesus who exists in human form because he has 'put on Adam' as a way of restoring the 'robe of glory to mankind'. [167]

Thy garment Lord is a fountain of healing, in thy visible dress dwells thy hidden power. [168]

The firstborn (Jesus) was clothed in the body, it was the veil of his glory. [169]

One of the most powerful and best known Christian uses of clothing as a metaphor for spiritual status occurs in the apocryphal Acts of Judas Thomas. The book is attributed to the apostle Thomas, an authorial uncertainty since it records his death. It contains strong Gnostic influences, and such heretical tendencies, together with its dubious authorship were probably sufficient to ensure that the book was excluded from the Christian Bible. Nevertheless it survives in the Christian Apocrypha. In the middle of the Acts of Thomas is an evocative and fascinating poem, but one which does not seem to be an original part of the book. Both the language and context suggest that it was written independently of this work, yet at some point in its history, an editor or perhaps even the compiler of the text felt that that the ode was sufficiently relevant to include in the book. Called The Hymn of the Pearl, it is the story of a young prince who is stripped of his royal garments and sent to Egypt to find a precious pearl. Should he return with it he will be restored to his former glory and royal stature.

The hymn is clearly Gnostic in character, the pearl representing wisdom, or gnosis, the ultimate Truth which it is the task of every initiate to attain. Egypt in Jewish and Christian tradition, is a netherworld, a place of servitude and bondage, and a necessary stopping place on the path to redemption. Thus in the Jewish tradition Jacob takes his family to Egypt to avoid famine; they are enslaved and emerge redeemed as Israel, to receive God's Torah on Mount Sinai. In Christianity, Jesus flees to Egypt to escape Herod and returns when the conditions are right for his redemptive mission. The hero of the Hymn of the Pearl can only find his redemption by seeking out and delivering the pearl of knowledge from Egypt.

When I was a little child, and dwelling in my kingdom, in my father's house ... my parents equipped me and sent me forth ...

And they took off from me the glittering robe, which in their affection they made for me, and the purple toga, which was measured and woven to my size. And they made a pact with me, and wrote it in my heart, that it might not be forgotten: 'If you go down into Egypt, and bring the one pearl, which is in the midst of the sea around the loud-breathing serpent, you shall put on your glittering robe and your toga...

I went down into Egypt ... I went straight to the serpent, I dwelt in his abode, waiting till he should slumber and sleep, and I could take my pearl from him ... And I put on their raiment, lest I should seem strange, as one that had come from abroad to recover the pearl; and lest the Egyptians should awake the serpent against me.

I began to charm him, the terrible loud breathing serpent. I hushed him asleep and lulled him into slumber ... And I snatched away the pearl ... And I stripped off the filthy garment and left it in their land, and directed my way forthwith to the light of my fatherland in the East ... And my bright robe, which I had stripped off, and the toga that was wrapped with it ... my parents had sent thither.

When I received it, the garment seemed to me to become like a mirror of myself ... my decorated robe, which was adorned with glorious colours, with gold and beryls and rubies and agates and sardonyxes, varied in colour. And it was skilfully worked in its home on high, and with diamond clasps were all its seams fastened; and the image of the king of kings was embroidered and depicted in full all over it, and like the stone of the sapphire too its hues were varied. And I saw also that all over it the instincts of knowledge were working, and I saw too that it was preparing to speak ... And in its kingly movements it poured itself entirely over me, and on the hand of its givers it hastened that I might take it. And love urged me to run to meet it and receive it; and I stretched forth and took it. With the beauty of its colours I adorned myself, and I wrapped myself wholly in my toga of brilliant hues. I clothed myself with it, and went up to the gate of salutation and prostration; I bowed my head and worshipped the majesty of my father who sent me ... for I had done his commandments, and he too had done what he promised ... And he promised that to the gate too of the king of kings with him I should go, and with my offering and my pearl with him should present myself to our king. [170]

The hero's garments in the Hymn of the Pearl symbolise his spiritual purity. He is obliged to remove his princely garments before he goes down to Egypt; whilst he is there he wears the filthy clothes of the land. Only when he has proved himself by slaying the serpent and obtaining the pearl, is he entitled to dress himself again in his original clothes. The whole hymn is a metaphor for the fall of humankind after Adam and Eve's original sin, with the descent to Egypt a parallel with the exile from the

Garden of Eden. The clothes that he leaves behind allude to special garments that that God made for Adam and Eve, whilst those that he puts on symbolise the gross materialism of this world. The pearl represents the truth that is awakened when Jesus arrives. Only when the young prince in the poem has the pearl can he return to his glory. Similarly, only after Jesus has redeemed the world can humankind once again restore itself to its original state, before what Christian theologians call the Fall of Man.

But to understand this better, and to discover the connection between the unstitched robe, which holds the key to the concealed agenda of the gospels, and the mythical garments that God makes for Adam and Eve, we need to turn our attention to the Garden of Eden story and the ancient Jewish legend of Adam and Eve's clothes.

8

The Legend of Adam's Clothes

At the beginning of Genesis, in the creation story, we read that following the expulsion of Adam and Eve from the garden of Eden.

God made garments of skin for Adam and his wife, and clothed them.[171]

We can use the midrashic principle of linking two or more passages which share a common word or phrase to connect the Hebrew word used here for garments, which is קתנת, pronounced *k'tonet*, with its Greek equivalent χιτων, in John 19,24 which describes the soldiers drawing lots over one of Jesus's garments.

The root of the Hebrew verb used in Genesis for 'clothed them', לבש, is the same as that used in Psalm 22,19 for the garment over which lots were drawn. The vocabulary of the verse in Genesis concerning the garments that God made for Adam and Eve therefore connects to both Psalm 22,19 and John 19,24. According to midrash, this allows us to establish a literary and contextual connection between the three passages and their respective sets of garments. The garment that the soldiers recognised as being holy, which they refused to divide, were related to the garments that God made for Adam and Eve.

This idea of a connection between Adam and Eve's clothes and Jesus's unstitched robe is supported by an early Syrian Christian text known as the Macarian Homilies. Although Macarian thought is not part of mainstream Christianity, there were times when it rose briefly to prominence within the church.

'I read Macarius and sang', wrote John Wesley in his diary for July 30, 1736. There are countless others alike in Eastern and in Western Christendom, who have experienced a similar joy through reading Macarius. The Homilies are written with a warmth of feeling, an affectivity and enthusiasm, that are instantly attractive. Their message is one of hope, light and glory.[172]

Little is known about the author of the Macarian Homilies. Scholars have dubbed him pseudo-Macarius, to distinguish him from other Macariuses who were known to early Christianity. Although he wrote in Greek, his style is Syrian, and the current opinion is that he was part of a heretical Christianity which came into conflict with the established church.

Macarius understands that Adam's garments represent God's glory, in which Adam is clothed. Needless to say Eve does not figure in this metaphor at all, as the early Christian world was as male centred as the Jewish environment from which it emerged.

Genesis 2,20 relates that Adam gave all the animals their names. We do not know how he acquainted himself with all the many animal species in order to do so, but according to an ancient biblical commentary, when the mighty hunter Nimrod, [173] builder of the Tower of Babel, wore Adam's clothes all the animals would fall before him.

Rabbi Judah said: The clothes that God made for Adam and Eve were with Noah in the ark. When they came out of the ark Noah's son Ham took them and brought them out and gave them to Nimrod. When he put them on, all the animals and beasts would fall before him. [174]

Did Adam's clothes – his elevated spiritual status – exercise some sort of power over the animals, enabling him to summon them, and give each one it its true, existential name? Macarius seems to hold this view:

As long as the Word of God was with him (Adam), he possessed everything. For the Word himself was his inheritance, his garment, and a glory that was his defence. It was his teaching. For it taught him how to give names to all things: 'Give this the name of heaven, that the sun; this the moon; that earth; this a bird; that a beast; that a tree.'[175]

To Macarius, the Word of God, or Spirit, is Adam's clothing. It is available as a garment to anyone who is a true believer in Jesus:

If anyone is naked and lacks the divine and heavenly garment which is the power of the Spirit ... let him weep and beg the Lord that he may receive from Heaven the spiritual garment ... God turns away from those who are not clothed with the garment of the Spirit with certainty, from those who have not 'put on the lord Jesus Christ' in power and in truth. [176]

All this might seem to be a bit obscure. But the reason we are dwelling on Macarius's philosophy of spiritual garments becomes clear in the next passage, where he claims that Jesus acquires the garments when he ascends the mountain with John and Peter, at the Transfiguration where he meets Moses and Elijah. Furthermore, this is the garment that he uses to perform his healing miracles:

... there appeared a splendid robe, such as not found anywhere in the whole world, not made by human hands. Just as when the lord ascended the mountain with John and Peter, he transformed his garments, making them brilliant like lightning, so too was that robe so that that man, clothed in it, was amazed and struck with awe. [177]

The believer should ... remember how the blind man was healed and how the woman with a haemorrhage likewise was healed by the touching of his garment. [178]

The incident of the haemorrhaging woman that Macarius refers to is related in the Gospel of Matthew:

And suddenly, a woman who had a flow of blood for twelve years came from behind and touched the hem of his garment. For she said to herself, 'If only I may touch his garment, I shall be made well.' But Jesus turned around, and when he saw her he said, 'Be of good cheer, daughter; your faith has made you well.' And the woman was made well from that hour. [179]

The unorthodox Syrian-Christian Macarius has attributed the healing miracles in the gospels to the fact that Jesus was wearing Adam's garments, acquired at the Transfiguration, when he met Moses and Elijah on the mountain. At times the Macarian garments are purely spiritual; a cloak which endows Adam with wisdom and the true believer with the power of the Spirit; but on Jesus they somehow fuse with his physical clothes, becoming transformed along with his face at the Transfiguration and possessing a healing quality for those who touch them.

Suddenly the threads are all starting to come together. When John hints at Jesus as wearing garments from heaven, he is alluding to this idea. The unstitched robe that Jesus wears on the cross represents Adam's clothes. And Adam's clothes, it turns out, have a history of their own that will explain why the unstitched robe became such a politically powerful symbol when Jesus wore it.

The story starts in Genesis when Isaac's wife Rebecca, wants her younger son Jacob, her favourite, to be given his father's blessing, in place of his older twin brother Esau, who is a disreputable character. But Isaac is fond of Esau and the only way she can engineer the blessing for Jacob is to encourage Jacob to dress as Esau, and imitate his behaviour, in order to deceive the nearly blind old man.

And Rebecca took the precious garments of her older son Esau which were with her in the house, and she placed them upon her younger son Jacob. [180]

The Aramaic translation Pseudo-Jonathan, which comments on the Bible by inserting extra, explanatory material, expands on this:

And Rebecca took Esau's precious garments that he had from Adam, for that day Esau had not put them on and they remained with her in the house, and she placed them upon her younger son Jacob[181].

According to this Hebrew legend Esau had somehow acquired Adam's clothes. Jacob comes into possession of them when his mother takes them from the older twin, Esau.

Much later in Jacob's life he explains to his own son Joseph how Esau obtained these garments. The Bible only alludes to this, but a legend which would have been known to the gospel writers fills in the gaps. In the Bible Jacob tells Joseph that:

I have given you an extra possession over your brothers... [182]

And an Aramaic translation, known as the Fragmentary Targum, which would have been similar to one known to the gospel writers, explains:

"And I have given you an extra possession over your brothers" means the garment of the first Adam: My grandfather Abraham, who took it from the hand of the wicked Nimrod, gave it to my father Isaac, my father Isaac gave it to Esau and I took it from the hand of my brother Esau... [183]

Another source adds an extra level of detail to the history of transmission of Adam's garments:

The first born used to offer sacrifices [on behalf of the community] before the tribe of Levi were appointed [as the priestly tribe]. Go back to the beginning of the world. Adam was the first born of the world. And when he offered a sacrifice he put on the garments of the High Priests, as the Bible says, 'God made garments of skin for Adam and his wife, and clothed them.' These were special garments which the first born wore to function as priests. When Adam died he gave them to Seth. Seth gave them to Methuselah who gave them to Noah ... Noah died and gave them to Shem [also known as Melchizedek]. As the Bible says, 'And Melchizedek, king of Shalem brought out bread and wine. [184] And he was the priest of the most high God ... Shem/Melchizedek died and gave them to Abraham ... he died and gave them to Isaac ... Isaac gave them to Jacob ...[185]

This midrash considers Adam's garments to be to be the uniform of the high priests. It claims to trace the pre-history of the Jewish priesthood, by outlining the chain of transmission of these garments from Adam to Abraham through a succession of early biblical characters. All the characters mentioned in this passage functioned as priests, because they all offered sacrifices – this is the ancient Hebrew definition of a priest. When they performed sacrificial rituals they wore the clothes that God made for Adam, for it was these garments that gave them the right to offer sacrifices. The office of priesthood had originally belonged to the first born, but we read in the book of Exodus that they lost this right following the episode of the golden calf, [186] when they participated in idol worship. From this point forward the entitlement to the priesthood was given to Moses's brother Aaron, a member of the tribe of Levi, which had not taken part in the worship of the golden calf.

And Moses stood in the gate of the camp and said 'Whoever is on God's side, come to me'; and all the tribe of Levi collected around him.[187]

And God said to Moses: See I have taken the Levites as my own from amongst the children of Israel, in place of the first born. [188]

Adam and Eve's garments are also discussed in a passage which quotes rabbis who lived during the 2nd and 3rd centuries:

In Rabbi Meir's copy of the Torah, instead of 'garments of skin', it read 'garments of light'. These were Adam's garments; similar to a lantern, wide beneath and narrow above. [189] *Rabbi Isaac the elder said they were as smooth as fingernails and as beautiful as pearls. Rabbi Yohanan said they were like the fine flax that comes from Bet Shean- they were called garments of skin because they clung to the skin. Rabbi Eleazar said made from goat-skin, Rabi Aibu said sheepskin, Rabbi Yehoshua ben Levi said, hare-skin, Rabbi Yose ben Hanina said skin and wool, Resh Lakish said like the work of heaven, and the firstborn would minister in them.* [190]

This source again links Adam and Eve's garments with the priestly function of the first born. The final view quoted is that they were 'like the work of heaven'. This is reminiscent of John's description of the tunic gambled over at the crucifixion which was 'from heaven'. Also, significantly, it shows that there was no 'official' view of what Adam and Eve's garments were. The suggestions range from the practical, different types of skins, to the ethereal, garments of light shaped like a lantern. Jewish tradition viewed the biblical account of the garments that God made for the first people as a hook on which to hang different ideas or principles. The idea that they were passed down through the generations as priestly garments was just one of the themes that was developed from them. Other, more mystical ideas emerged from the view that they were not physical clothes at all, but garments of light.

The Holy Grail and Joseph's many coloured coat

The last that we hear of Adam's garments is when Jacob has them, long before the Jewish priesthood was formally established. After this different biblical characters wear distinctive clothes to display their status, but they are no longer referred to as Adam's garments.

The most famous of all biblical clothing is almost certainly Joseph's coat of many colours. 'Many coloured' is a poor translation of the Hebrew word which is pronounced *passim*. A better rendering would be 'coat of pieces', or 'patchwork coat'. But, as with the exact nature of Adam's garments, ancient Hebrew tradition was divided as to the precise meaning of the Hebrew phrase:

A coat of pieces [passim]: Because its sleeves reached the palm (pas) of his hand. Another explanation: Because it was extremely thin and light and could be concealed in the palm of his hand. Another explanation: Because they drew lots [paysim] over it to see which of them would bring it to their father. And the lot fell on Judah. [191]

According to the final view in this passage Joseph's coat was a 'coat of lottery' because of Joseph's brothers, who had cast him into the pit and dipped his coat in goat's blood to make it appear that he had been devoured by wild animals. The brothers drew lots over the coat, in order to decide which of them would report to their father the untruth that they had found it torn by the roadside.

Joseph's coat had been made for him by his father as a sign of his special affection. The twelfth of Jacob's thirteen children, he was the eldest son of Jacob's most beloved wife Rachel. By giving him a special garment, Jacob formalised Joseph's position as his principal heir, even though he was not the oldest brother. The garment invested Joseph with the status of leader; it was effectively a robe of office.

Joseph's passage into Egypt is the seminal event which leads directly to the establishment of Israel as an independent nation, adhering to a new monotheistic religion. The language of the Bible first emphasises the progressive *descent* of Joseph, into the pit, into Egypt, and finally into prison. As his fortunes change, the language becomes that of *ascent* – out of prison, to the position of viceroy and, in time out of the land itself. In a similar vein Christianity speaks of Jesus's descent into flesh, and rising from the tomb.

Joseph is betrayed by his brothers for twenty pieces of silver. [192] It was his brother Judah who advocated the sale, arguing that there was no profit in merely killing him. Jesus is betrayed by one of his spiritual brothers for thirty pieces of silver. [193] The betrayal was carried out by Judas, which is a Greek form of Judah.

Joseph was imprisoned in Egypt because he resisted his mistress's advances. He tells her that he is unable to do as she wishes, because it would be a betrayal of his master's trust and 'I would sin against God.'[194] His refusal was therefore not due to a lack of desire; it was a religious imperative, of a similar quality to Jesus's lifelong self-denial.

Both Jesus and Joseph feed the masses. Jesus, miraculously, by enabling five thousand people to dine on five loaves and two fish. Joseph, politically, feeds the entire Egyptian nation by carefully managing the storage and sale of food. We can see echoes of the events in Joseph's life in the later stories told about Jesus.

We might ask why Jacob goes to the trouble of making a coat for Joseph instead of passing on Adam's clothes to him. All the sources that discuss the line of transmission of Adam's clothes, stop at Jacob. Instead of passing them onto Joseph he makes him a new, special garment. Thus Joseph's many coloured coat, or coat of lottery, replaces Adam's clothes.

Adam's clothes that God had made for him vanish with Jacob, but their significance, their inherited, divine quality becomes attached to Joseph's coat. He is placed firmly in the line of transmission of Adam's garments, without actually having to possess them. For Adam's garments, like Adam himself, were flawed. At times they ended up in the wrong hands; the wicked Nimrod and Esau had each managed to get hold of them, and used their hypnotic influence (which Adam had used to name the animals, and Noah no doubt had used to summon the beasts to the Ark) to hunt and kill for their own personal pleasure. By making a new garment, one without a history and with a destiny of its own, Jacob is trying to ensure that he passes the baton onto his favoured son, without any risk that the flawed nature of Adam's garments may cause them to end up with another, less favoured brother. As had happened to him when Esau got hold of them.

Sadly, Jacob's plan does not work, Joseph's brothers rip his coat from him, dip it in blood and send it back to their father. They knew that this coat symbolised the special divine favour that had been handed down through the generations from Adam, and which in turn had been passed by their father to Joseph. They weren't going to be fooled. Realising that that their father intended them to play second fiddle to Joseph, they throw him in the pit and destroy the coat. Joseph gets carted off to Egypt where, following a complex array of divinely orchestrated events he eventually ends up as prime minister. In due course his father and brothers join him to escape a famine in their homeland. Their descendants remain in the country, growing in number and power until the Egyptians fear the alien hoard in their midst. The Egyptian king, pharaoh turns against them and the Israelites end up as an enslaved people, which is the last we hear of any special clothes until years later, when they finally leave Egypt.

But when the Israelites do finally leave Egypt and attain the status of an independent nation, Moses, under God's direction establishes a social structure for the wandering population. He hands the principal function of high priest to his brother Aaron. At this point garments reappear within the biblical narrative.

They occur in chapter twenty-eight of Exodus which announces Aaron's appointment, and designates his sons to assist him. It describes in vivid, expanded detail the new priestly garments that were to be manufactured, and to be worn whenever the priests carried out their duties. These were tailored by skilled artisans, from wools, fabrics, dyes, jewels, and precious metals, all freely donated by the people. The priestly garments were indispensable; a priest who did not wear them invalidated the ritual that he was participating in. The garments invested the wearer with a special sanctity; they were not just decorations, but provided the priest with the spiritual elevation necessary to perform his task.

A ceremony was necessary to induct Aaron, the first high priest, into office. This could only be carried out by someone of a superior status, who could appoint him to office. In other words another high priest. This was a chicken and egg moment; there were no other priests, the firstborn had been deposed following their misdemeanour with the golden calf. Where would they find a high priest to inaugurate the first high priest?

The only person in Israel who had the authority to step into the breach and consecrate Aaron as high priest was his brother Moses. Chapter eight of Leviticus describes in detail the ceremony that Moses performed when Aaron was consecrated as high priest, and his sons inducted as deputy priests.

According to Leviticus Moses performed priestly rituals at Aaron's ordination ceremony.[195] He temporarily functioned as a priest, according to the Jewish definition, just long enough to consecrate Aaron's new order of priesthood.

Because of the great attention that Judaism paid to the design and manufacture of its priestly garments, we would expect that when Moses inducted Aaron into office, he too would wear distinctive clothes. Indeed the Talmud records the following discussion:

Mar Ukba was asked...in which garments did Moses minister during the seven days of consecration [during which Aaron was ordained]. He was unable to answer. He went and inquired in the academy and was told ... Moses ministered in a white robe. Rav Kahana taught: In a white robe that was unstitched. [196]

Mar Ukba and Rav Kahana both lived in Babylon in the first half of the 3rd century, a century or more after John. Another version of this incident has the same question being asked of Rabbi Akiba, who died in the year 135. If Akiba was enquiring in the academy it is likely that the answer he was given dated back even earlier than John. Even if the authentic version is that of Mar Ukba we still have an early, almost contemporaneous account of Moses consecrating a new order of priests, wearing an unstitched robe, exactly the same as that which John has the soldiers drawing lots over at the crucifixion; a white robe.

Jesus's robe becomes white following the Transfiguration, and John tells us as part of the crucifixion narrative that it is unstitched; Moses too puts on a white, unstitched robe to inaugurate his brother into the priesthood.

Moses's white unstitched robe empowered him to inaugurate a hierarchy of priests. Jesus's white, unstitched robe, the Holy Grail, intended him to perform a similar function. And this intention to empower a new order of priests, to serve in the Jerusalem Temple is the key to understanding Jesus's political agenda.

9

The Significance of the Grail

Both the Hebrew and Christian bibles communicate ideas through symbol and metaphor. Both Joseph's coat of lottery and the holy grail are symbolic representations of Adam's clothes. Joseph's coat was ripped from him by his brothers, who drew lots to decide who would send it back to their father. As a result it vanishes from history. The author of John's gospel knew this and he wasn't going to have the same thing happen to Jesus's coat of lottery.

> *Then the soldiers, when they had crucified Jesus, took ... the tunic ... they said ...'Let us not tear it.'*

A literate bible reader in gospel times would get the allusion to Joseph's coat immediately.

The gospels recount how Jesus's garments are transformed into the Holy Grail as a result of a supernatural event, the Transfiguration. They become identical to the garments worn by Moses when he invests his brother Aaron with the eternal priesthood. The grail therefore comes to symbolise the divinely-awarded power to consecrate a new priesthood. We can understand this if we compare it to the sceptre which symbolised authority or kingship in the ancient world.

> *This sceptre Achaea's sons take in hand whenever they do justice in Zeus' name*[197]
>
> *The sceptre shall not depart from Judah, nor a law scribe from between his feet*[198].

There is a bizarre, obscure passage tucked away in one of the lighter sections of the Talmud which parodies heathen religious ceremonies carried out in foreign lands.

Rav Yehuda, quoting Shmuel said 'The Romans have another ceremony: Once every seventy years they bring a healthy man and make him ride on a lame man. They dress him in the garments that Adam wore and place on his head the skull of Rabbi Ishmael. They place a weight of precious gold around his neck and cover the markets with it, proclaiming before him: The son of the Lord is false.'[199]

This is a strange passage for a number of reasons, and we have to accept the possibility that it may have been corrupted or censored in some way. The medieval church establishment frequently demanded the censorship of Jewish religious texts which they felt undermined their faith, and if they didn't censor books they often destroyed them. In June 1242 twenty four wagon loads of the Talmud were burnt in Paris on the orders of Pope Gregory. Thousands of volumes, in an age before printing had been invented, were lost. This, together with natural wastage has meant that only one full version of the Talmud, known as the Munich codex, has survived into modern times. All of which makes it difficult to establish the true pre-censored version of any Talmudic text. Nevertheless, in the absence of any evidence to the contrary, we can only take the passage at face value.

Shmuel, in whose name the passage is quoted, lived in Babylon during the first half of the 3rd century, in the period before the Roman empire adopted Christianity, and at a time when the Romans were heavily persecuting Christians. The proclamation that 'the son of the Lord is false' suggests that the Roman ceremony being described was a deliberate denigration of Christianity. This is supported by the reference to the lame man and the healthy man. Jesus is often referred to in the Talmud by the code name Balaam, to avoid the censor's pen. The original Balaam was a biblical prophet whose mission was to curse Israel. One Jewish source[200] considers his level of prophecy to be on a par with Moses, and in some respects to be even greater. In order to teach controversial subjects to their students, the Talmudic rabbis often spoke in coded language. In Jewish literature Balaam is described as being lame. This is based on Numbers 23,3 where Balaam is described as walking haltingly. The lame man in the Roman ceremony is therefore a deliberate, and recognisable allusion to Balaam who in turn, as a great prophet of another faith, was a suitable codename for Jesus.

The symbolic role of Jesus in the ceremony may have been played by a Christian slave. The healthy man wore a chain of gold – signifying status and prosperity. Rabbi Ishmael, with whose skull he was crowned was a former Jewish high priest, executed by the Romans during the period of destruction of the Jerusalem Temple.

But most importantly for our purposes is that the passage has Jesus's conqueror dressed in Adam's clothes. They obviously weren't Adam's real clothes, which are the stuff of mythology. But they possibly included the genuine unstitched robe which had found its way to Rome with the soldier who had won it in the lottery. The Roman ceremony which the Jewish Talmud describes, may have been a ritual involving the Holy Grail which was now featuring in a patriotic Roman charade.

The Holy Grail appears to have been of sufficient importance to the early Christians that it was a natural symbol for the Romans to include in their parody. Further the fact of the parody itself suggests that the threat that Christianity posed to the Romans was more than just that of an alien religion. After all, the Roman empire dominated the known world. There would have been hosts of different religious practices within its borders. Why did the Romans choose to pick on this one. Indeed, why did they persecute Christians at all? Granted, the time did come when Constantine converted the empire to Christianity, and during the period leading up to that transformation there would have been many who resisted it. But the Talmudic passage about the lame man was quoted two centuries before this. It was the unholy and dangerous convergence of a struggle for political and religious power in a backwater province that made Rome sit up and take notice.

Priests and Politics

The wearer of the grail, the white unstitched robe of the Transfiguration, divided by lottery at the crucifixion, symbolic heir of Moses's authority, possessed the power to inaugurate priests. These priests were the link between the world in which people lived, and the great unknown beyond. Where ordinary people walked in ignorance, priests knew the mind of God. They could heal the sick, bring down the rains, bestow blessing, impose curses, exorcise demons, remove sin, and cleanse souls.

To provide them with sustenance was to bring a blessing upon oneself and one's family. To disobey was to risk untold punishment and suffering.

In ancient times the priests were the educated classes. One of the earliest responsibilities that they were given, prescribed in the Mosaic book of Leviticus was to examine people who were feared to be suffering from leprosy, and to prescribe a complex process of isolation and re-examination until the disease was confirmed one way or the other. [201] This presupposes at the least a rudimentary understanding of primitive medicine. Centuries later, following the Israelites' return from forced exile in Babylon in 458 BCE, Ezra the priest instituted the public reading of the Torah as the primary means of educating the people back into their religion. It was the priests' role to perform the public reading. They were the educated and the educators. Additionally, they were the keepers of arcane mysteries, scrupulously parcelled up and transmitted to different priestly families for safe keeping. Only one family knew the secret formulae for manufacturing the Temple incense, another kept the recipe for the oil of anointing, and only the high priest himself was able to pronounce the unutterable name of God. [202]

Modern Western religions are practised in local places of worship. Ordinary people are able to attend, take part in prayers and celebrate the festivals. Everyone who feels so inclined has the opportunity to enter into a personal relationship with the divinity. One does not need to come from a particular family, tribe, or caste to join the clergy.

Ancient Judaism was not like this, Rather, it was what is known as a cultic religion. Its rituals took place in a central Temple, in Jerusalem and religious activity was conducted by priests, on behalf of the entire nation. Although the ordinary population would have celebrated the festivals and sabbaths, they were not ritually involved. They did not play a substantial role in the religious ceremonies. There were few private prayers, which individuals would recite alone. Personal benedictions and supplications were secondary events which accompanied the various Temple rituals, performed by the priests. There were some synagogues, but their function was limited. The people would go to the Temple in Jerusalem to watch the various rituals, but they were spectators; it was the priests, and their assistants the Levites, who actually performed the rites on behalf of the entire community.

The priesthood was a hereditary office. Aaron, Moses's brother was the first high priest, and after his death the role passed to his son Eliezer, thence to his son Pinchas and downwards to the firstborn son of each generation. Alongside the high priest there were the ordinary priests, members of the same family who were not part of the firstborn line. Ministering to them were the Levites, the other members of the same tribe who were not direct descendants of Aaron.

In time, and particularly as we approach Jesus's time, the high priest's hereditary lineage became corrupted; the office was sold and resold amongst the wealthy and the powerful. This is one of the reasons that Jesus wanted to institute his own, reformed priesthood.

The Destruction of the Temple

When the Romans destroyed Jerusalem, after a century of occupation, they looted its Temple, set fire to the building and carried its bounty off to Rome. A triumphal arch was erected in Rome, in honour of the Emperor Titus and in celebration of his victory over the Jews. One of its faces fronts the Coliseum; the other, the Forum. A bas-relief on the arch shows Jewish slaves, or possibly Roman soldiers- the definition is no longer clear, carrying the spoils of the Temple of Jerusalem. The articles depicted on the arch are the two tablets of the Law fastened on staffs, the seven-branched candlestick, and the golden table on which were placed the sacred trumpets. There is a tradition in Rome that no Jew ever passed under this arch. Why would they, since it depicted the destruction of the glory of their nation?

With the destruction of the Temple, Judaism was shaken to its roots. It wasn't simply that the religion could not function because it no longer had a centre in which to practice its rituals. The destruction affected the civil life of the country as well and was a national crisis of unprecedented proportions. The Temple was not just the religious focus of Israel, but was also the political and legal centre, the life blood of the nation. It was the home of the supreme law courts which also functioned as the legislative authority, within whatever limits the Roman governor would permit. Whilst the Romans allowed the Temple to stand, the Jewish state could use its independent religious centre as an umbrella within which to conduct matters of national and political concern. Once the Temple fell, it was not just the religion, but the nation itself, which appeared to be doomed.

The emergence of modern Judaism as a home and synagogue based, quasi-democratic faith, represents one of the most revolutionary events in the history of world religion. A group of far sighted scholars, known as Pharisees, responded to the seriousness of the situation with outstanding creativity. Over a relatively short period of time they replaced a Temple based, sacrificial, cultic institution with a populist, participative religion that also managed to jettison the need for, and privileges accorded to, the priestly caste.

They did this by taking the scholarship, knowledge, and traditions which had resided in the priestly families and amongst the educated lay classes for centuries, and transmitting them to the population at large. The Pharisees empowered the people by teaching them what to do and how to do it. As part of this process, they got rid of defunct practices that the forces of conservatism would never have abandoned and opened up education and opportunity to the masses. They debated fiercely amongst themselves, in the academies and on the streets. Originally they committed nothing to writing; everything was memorised and communicated orally. This allowed the teachings and faith to develop organically and not become fossilised.

To give their teachings authority they rooted their traditions in the Bible. They developed the belief that when God gave the Ten Commandments and the rest of the Torah to Moses on Mount Sinai he also transmitted a verbal interpretation of the laws, which would be developed and expanded generation by generation. The idea was that alongside the written, unchanging Bible there would exist an ever-evolving, organic body of knowledge rooted in the past but flexible enough to respond to any eventuality in the future. Since this body of knowledge would be transmitted by word of mouth it would have in-built flexibility. It was intended to be dynamic, adapting subtly but effectively to social and technological change. Unlike the Ten Commandments, it would not be rooted in stone.

But times change and as the Roman grip on the country grew stronger, and the people became more oppressed and demotivated, there was an increased danger of the oral traditions becoming forgotten. The students of the original Pharisees, now known as rabbis, collated and edited their teachings, wrote them down, then began to debate them again. The first recension of the teachings became known as the Mishnah, and the subsequent debates were recorded some centuries later, in the Talmud.

It took time for the new system to evolve and stabilise. In the meantime the destruction of the Temple had put serious strain on the Jewish belief system. To the religious mind it seemed obvious that the events were a punishment for the sins of the nation against God. The rabbis blamed the calamity on 'causeless hatred' in society. They used their powerful sense of narrative and metaphor to graphically illustrate the scale of political and social breakdown that must have existed. Social breakdown that was rooted in seemingly insignificant, petty hatred:

Rabbi Yohanan said: 'The destruction of Jerusalem came through Kamza and Bar Kamza. A certain man had a friend called Kamza and an enemy called Bar Kamza. He once made a party and said to his servant, "Go and bring Kamza." The man accidentally brought Bar Kamza. When the host found him there he said "You slander me, what are you doing here? Get out." Said the other: "Since I am here, let me stay, and I will pay you for whatever I eat and drink." He said, "I will not." "Then let me give you half the cost of the party." "No", said the other. "Then let me pay for the whole party." He still said, "No", and he seized him by the hand and threw him out. Said Bar Kamza, "Since the Rabbis were sitting there and did not stop him, this shows that they agreed with him. I will go and inform against them, to the (Roman) Government." He went and said to the Emperor, "The Jews are rebelling against you." He said, "How can I know this?" He said to him: "Send them an offering and see whether they will offer it on the altar." So the Emperor sent him off with a fine calf. As Bar Kamza was leading the animal along the way he made a blemish on its upper lip[203]... The Rabbis were inclined to offer it in order not to offend the Government. Said Rabbi Zechariah ben Abkulas to them: "People will say that blemished animals are offered on the altar"'... Rabbi Yohanan thereupon remarked: 'Through the scrupulousness of Rabbi Zechariah ben Abkulas our House has been destroyed, our Temple burnt and we ourselves exiled from our land.' [204]

A major consequence of the destruction of the Temple was the loss of political power by the priests. According to biblical law the priests were not supposed to own land, but as is so often the case with organised religious establishments, the priestly families had developed into a prosperous and politically influential aristocracy. Prosperous because their daily needs were taken care of by the sacrifices donated to the Temple and by tithes brought by farmers and peasants. Politically influential due to the continuous presence that they maintained in Jerusalem, the capital and centre of all economic activity.

The wealthiest and most influential group amongst the priests, the patricians in the Roman social model, were known as the Sadducees. The name comes from the high priestly family in Solomon's original Temple, built in 960 BCE. The founder of this family, Zadok, traced his ancestry back to Pinchas, Aaron's grandson, who had been rewarded by God with the eternal priesthood.

But round about the time of Jesus the Sadducees, like many aristocracies, started to grow complacent. The masses favoured the more meritocratic and egalitarian approach of the Pharisees and supported their efforts to gain political and religious influence. Power began to shift from the Sadducees to the Pharisees. The reason why the Pharisees receive such a bad press in the Christian Bible is because their attempts to rebuild Judaism conflicted with the efforts of the Jewish founders of Christianity to promote their ideas.

The rivalries between the Pharisees, who became the majority group and won the support of the bulk of the population, and the Jewish Christians influenced the attitudes of the gospels. The gospels were set thirty years before the destruction of the Temple but were not finally edited until well after. By this time the early Christians – still Jews by descent and family tradition – had started to preach beyond the borders of Israel, to the Roman territories around the Mediterranean. They were, however, losing the battle for the religious soul of the people of Israel themselves, and to their minds it was the fault of the Pharisees. This explains texts in Matthew like:

> *Then the Pharisees went out and plotted against him, how they might destroy him.* [205]
>
> *Woe to you, scribes and Pharisees, hypocrites! For you travel land and sea to win one convert, and when he is won, you make him twice as much a son of hell as yourselves.* [206]

But although the Pharisees were able to institute reforms in the Jewish religion which enabled it to flourish in the absence of a Temple, this did not mean that they despaired of ever seeing the Temple rebuilt. Far from it. Their prayers, hopes and dreams were all towards the restoration of the Temple cult and the return of the Jewish faith to former glories. Which worried the Romans.

The Roman mockery of the Holy Grail and Christianity all stemmed from centuries long concern about what might happen in the rebellious Jewish province of Palestine should the discredited and disempowered Temple priesthood ever manage to regain its influence amongst the Jews.

Early Christianity and the Jewish Priesthood

The destruction of the Temple, political turmoil, and spiritual angst combined to create a set of conditions ripe for a succession of quick-fix preachers and groups to emerge with their own religious solutions. Not so different from the Western world today, a world in which organised religion has by and large broken down, and in which new, alternative philosophies compete with each other, and fads and fleetingly fashionable solutions emerge for the attention of those seeking instant answers, truth or comfort.

Christianity developed from this melting pot of ideas, along with the teachings of many other preachers and prophets, now long forgotten. While the rabbis of the time were creating what became known as rabbinic Judaism, other groups including the founders of various different sects and strains of Christianity, reacted to the sense of national crisis with their own dogmas.

Jesus and his disciples, were observant, if free-thinking, Jews and the Jewish priesthood was an integral element in their religious background. Far from setting out to create a new religion, the early Christians were a reforming group within an established Judaism that was already undergoing a major upheaval. They did not just encourage adherence to the law of Moses, they urged their followers to be even more spiritually upright than the existing religious establishment.

Do not think that I came to destroy the Law or the Prophets. I did not come to destroy but to fulfil. For assuredly, I say to you, till heaven and earth pass away, not one jot or tittle[207] will pass from the law till all is fulfilled. Whoever therefore breaks one of the least of these commandments, [208] and teaches men so, shall be called least in the kingdom of heaven; but whoever does and teaches them, he shall be called great in the kingdom of heaven. For I say to you, that unless your righteousness exceeds the righteousness of the scribes and Pharisees, you will by no means enter the kingdom of heaven.
209

One of the central questions for Jesus and his followers, as a reformist group, would have been how their new approach to Judaism interacted with the established priesthood who, despite the fact their own power was waning, still held sway.

If the Christians were to succeed in reforming Judaism, to create a new Israel, they would need to integrate the priests. Provided they had the religious influence they required, the early Christians would have been content with a Judaism which kept its basic infrastructure, with a Temple in which sacrifices were offered, and a priesthood drawn from the traditional families. Their early intentions were simply to replace what they saw as the strict legalism of Judaism with the more spiritual approach that forms the core of the gospel messages. This is clearly stressed in early Christian works such as the epistle of Barnabas, which encourages devotion to the Jewish Bible but by emphasising the spiritual aspect of the commandments over their intricate observance.

> *Let us become spiritual, let us become a Temple perfect unto God. As far as in us lies, let us exercise ourselves in the fear of God, and let us strive to keep his commandments, that we may rejoice in His ordinances.* [210]

10

Revolution in the Temple

The Christians were a popular movement, and growing in influence daily. They had supporters in the Temple and amongst the aristocracy. John mentions Nicodemus, an officiating priest who was sympathetic to the Christian cause [211], and there is the account of Jesus's relationship with the wealthy Lazarus and Mary[212]:

> *Six days before the Passover, Jesus arrived at Bethany, where Lazarus lived, whom Jesus had raised from the dead. Here a dinner was given in Jesus's honour. Martha served, while Lazarus was among those reclining at the table with him. Then Mary took about a pint of pure nard, an expensive perfume; she poured it on Jesus's feet and wiped his feet with her hair. And the house was filled with the fragrance of the perfume. But one of his disciples, Judas Iscariot, who was later to betray him, objected, 'Why wasn't this perfume sold and the money given to the poor? It was worth a year's wages.'* [213]

Jesus's followers knew that during the course of the previous century and a half religious political authority had been shifting from the Sadducees to the Pharisees, to a point where the Pharisaic party could now be confident of popular support whilst the aristocratic, priestly Sadducees were on the defensive, their position bolstered by the Romans. It looked at the time as if the Christians could engineer a further shift in power, oust the Pharisees and reform Judaism in their own mould.

It was unlikely, however, that they could do this through the established seat of power, the Sanhedrin, the ultimate civic body, parliament and supreme court rolled into one. The Sanhedrin was dominated by Pharisees, and although there were Sadducee members, the body's own constitution protected it from infiltration by outside elements. The seventy-one member Sanhedrin was the national council of sages, and members were appointed for life. When one died the council themselves would appoint a replacement, an emerging sage whose learning was already respected, and who generally conformed to the religious and social philosophy of the dominant Pharisee party – although there always remained a small Sadducean minority. A new member's seat would be in one of the rear rows in the semi circular chamber. As he grew older, and more senior members passed away, he advanced through the ranks, moving closer and closer to the centre of power in the front row. The idea of the new Christians getting enough people onto the Sanhedrin in the current climate was unworkable. It was far more practical to seek influence through the largely discredited priesthood.

The priesthood had started to come off the rails over a century earlier, when a family of priests, the Hasmoneans, had unconstitutionally proclaimed themselves monarchs. This was contrary to all Jewish juridical principles; ever since the earliest days there had been a separation between religion and state, a position that was one of the fundamental guarantees of a stable society. Nevertheless, between 166 and 163 BCE, the Hasmoneans who had successfully led the national revolt against the Greek-Syrian invaders and regained political freedom for Israel, established themselves as the monarchy. It may have been unconstitutional but it was better than being occupied by the Greeks. There was little outcry from the people and the Hasmonean dynasty rapidly became a fait accompli. The rule of the Hasmonean priest-kings finally came to an end with the onset of the Roman occupation and their name all but disappeared from history. Yet, despite attempts by the other Sadducean families to restore the high priesthood to its former integrity, the office never recovered. High priests would often serve for just a year at a time, in rotation, rather than for life in accordance with the biblical prescription; at times there was more than one high priest. [214] The system had collapsed, power could be purchased and the populace often had little regard for its priestly leaders. Popular dissent against the priests surfaced regularly:

It happened with a high priest that as he came forth from the Sanctuary, all the people followed him, but when they saw Shemayah and Abtalion, [215] they left him and went after them. Finally Shemayah and Abtalion came across to the high priest, to take their leave of him. He said to them: May the foreigners[216] come in peace! — They answered him: The foreigners will come in peace for they do the work of Aaron but the descendant of Aaron[217] shall not come in peace for he does not do the work of Aaron. [218]

Once [a high priest] poured the libation water upon his feet [instead of the altar] and all the people stoned him with their citrons.[219]

In 1973 Hyam Maccoby published his provocative work *Revolution in Judea*. Maccoby shows the extent to which the priesthood was subservient to Rome, and the depth of disdain which it evoked amongst the people at large.

The High Priest was a Sadducee and it is one of the most important points to grasp in New Testament studies that the High Priest was appointed by the Romans. As a member of a quisling minority group he was regarded with contempt by the great mass of the nation. Religious authority lay not with the priests but with an entirely different body of people called the Rabbis, who were the leaders of the Pharisees....The resistance against Rome came from the Pharisee party. [220]

If it was possible for the high priesthood to be obtained by wealthy men with influence amongst the aristocracy and with the Roman government, it was conceivable that a charismatic leader could attain it through popular acclaim, particularly if he could demonstrate the appropriate level of spiritual leadership. This would have been the ideal scenario for the early Christians.

But Jesus was not a member of the priestly tribe. He claimed descent from the royal House of David. This underlies the entire political-messianic agenda of the gospels. The opening sentence in the first chapter of the Christian Bible, (the Gospel of Matthew), traces Jesus's ancestry back to David. The last act in his life, is the Roman governor, Pilate, erecting a sign at the crucifixion proclaiming Jesus as the King of the Jews. [221]

Jesus could not influence the priesthood from within because he was not a priest. Furthermore, as a member of the royal household, a descendant of David, he could not even consider appropriating the priesthood for himself. This would have been to commit the same error as the Hasmoneans, something the people would not have stood for. To be sure, the priesthood is exactly what Pauline Christianity claimed for Jesus but that was later, following the destruction of the priests' seat of power in the Temple, and to a different audience. The political climate was very different then.

The desire to find a synthesis between the spiritual teachings of early Christianity and the existing priestly establishment grew less urgent following the destruction of the Temple and the growing awareness that it would not be speedily rebuilt. Post-destruction Christianity, planning to become the Jewish mainstream, no longer needed to worry about how to interact with the now irrelevant, largely defunct, Jewish priesthood.

Jesus himself could not be a priest, but the priesthood was an institution in need of new, invigorated leadership. It would be an ideal power base if Jesus and his followers could find a way to exert influence over it. The priests could be an authentic conduit for his teachings to reach the people. Whereas the Pharisees, the main religious opposition party, were in the process of bypassing the priesthood, through the establishment of a democratic system of rabbis, or teachers, Jesus's solution was to reinvigorate and reform the priesthood itself.

For the priest's lips should guard knowledge, and they should seek the Torah from his mouth...[222]

As a member of the tribe of Judah, Jesus could not become a priest in the Jewish Temple. Nor, for political reasons, could he and his followers be appointed to the Sanhedrin. His options were limited. Although his avenues for movement may have been restricted, his supporters had more flexibility and could move around more freely. There was a route open to them. All that was needed was to frame a strategy in such as way as to resonate with the cultural expectations of their audience.

A close reading of the gospels suggests a deliberate policy on the part of Jesus and his followers to become involved in Temple life. They used both education and confrontation to influence the religious attitudes of the worshippers and priestly officials in the Temple. The gospels portray Jesus using the Temple as a venue in which to teach. They do not spell out the significance of this, even though it brought him into conflict with the priestly authorities:

Now when he came into the Temple, the chief priests and the elders of the people confronted him as he was teaching, and said, 'By what authority are you doing these things? And who gave you this authority?'[223]

Although the scribes and rabbis had taken over the educational function by the time of Jesus, the Temple remained the religious centre of the nation. Great scholars and rabbis taught there. When he too taught in the Temple, Jesus staked his claim to be regarded as one of the principal educators in Israel.

We have seen how Jesus becomes involved in a confrontation in the temple, during which he claims that the law prohibiting healing on the Sabbath is illogical.

> *Now about the middle of the feast Jesus went up into the Temple and taught. And the Jews marvelled, saying, 'How does this man know the law, having never studied?' Jesus answered them and said, 'My doctrine is not mine, but His who sent me. If anyone wants to do His will, he shall know concerning the doctrine, whether it is from God or whether I speak on my own authority ... Did not Moses give you the law ... ? I performed one act of work, and you all marvel. Moses gave you circumcision ... and you circumcise a man on the Sabbath. If a man receives circumcision on the Sabbath ... are you angry with me because I made a man completely well on the Sabbath?* [224]

This confrontation is not just recorded in the gospels, but also, in coded form, in the Jerusalem Talmud, which is less known but older than the Babylonian Talmud. In keeping with its style, the Jerusalem Talmud uses this confrontation to explain a difficult passage in the Jewish Bible. We read in the book of Numbers that a dispute breaks out in the wilderness between Moses and his cousin Korah. The Talmud imagines a conversation between the two which it suggests lies at the heart of their falling out. In this conversation Korah notes that Moses has commanded that the garments of the Jews should have a fringe of blue-dyed thread attached to each corner, and that the door of every house should have a parchment on it containing a particular passage from the Bible:

> *Korah made a garment that was dyed blue throughout. He came to Moses. 'Moses our teacher, if a garment is completely dyed blue, does it still need a blue-dyed thread on each corner?' Moses replied*

'Yes it does need a fringe.' Korah retorted 'What about a house that is full of Bible scrolls, does it need a parchment on the door[225]? He replied 'Yes.' Korah said: This is not God's law and Moses is not a prophet. [226]

The debate between Moses and Korah is in essence the same as that between Jesus and the people. Both Korah and Jesus bring examples of logical inconsistencies in Moses's law and use the principle of argument *ad majus*, known in midrashic terminology as *kal v'homer*, to prove their point. But Korah was not just any disputatious Israelite. His claim to fame is that he too was a Levite, from a more senior family than Moses, and he was jealous that Moses and his brother Aaron had shared both religious and temporal power between them.

And Moses said to Korah: 'Hear now, you sons of Levi; is it a small thing to you, that the God of Israel has separated you from the congregation of Israel ... to stand before the congregation to minister to them ... and all your brothers the sons of Levi with you that you also seek the priesthood?[227]

Korah had led a rebellion against Moses in the wilderness in an attempt to gain the priesthood for himself and his followers. When the compilers of the Jerusalem Talmud put an argument into his mouth that was similar to one that Jesus had used, they were doing this deliberately. They were aware that Jesus had sought influence within the priesthood for his followers – his agenda may in time have been excised from Pauline Christianity but the Jews had no reason to cover it up. On the other hand they did not wish to make much of a fuss about it, as by the time the Talmud was written the Roman Empire had officially adopted Christianity. So the Talmudic editors transmitted their message by means of a cipher. They used the biblical example of Korah's priestly revolt to illustrate something similar that had happened centuries earlier, the attempt by Jesus to reform the Temple institutions.

The other famous Temple confrontation that Jesus gets involved in is when he upsets the tables of the money changers and drives them from the Temple. As we have noted, this is not the action of a man trying to overthrow Judaism, but of a strong leader seeking to implement reform.

Sinister Influences

So far the evidence suggests that Jesus wanted to reform a Temple priesthood that had become complacent and irrelevant. But other passages imply that this process of reform was not wholly benign. An apparently casual reference in a strange and frequently overlooked passage occurring in all four gospels has a more sinister feel to it.

When Jesus is arrested, the gospels almost parenthetically record that a fight took place, during which the apostle Peter cuts off the right ear of the high priest's servant. Fighting and violence seem to be the very antithesis of everything that the apostles stood for and the passage cries out for investigation.

John adds that the servant's name was Malchus. The name Malchus in Hebrew means kingdom. The Talmud described Jesus as 'near to Malchus'[228], meaning that he was related to royalty, i.e. the Davidic line. Naming the high priest's servant Malchus is almost certainly a coded metaphor to indicate that the kingdom, meaning political power, had been appropriated by the high priest. It implied that the royal household ministered to the priesthood. This had been the historical reality before the Roman conquest when the Hasmonean priests declared themselves kings. Malchus, the kingdom, had become subordinate to the priesthood.

The high priest, when he was inducted into office, had sacrificial blood sprinkled upon the tip of his right ear[229]. By slicing off the right ear of the high priest's servant, the kingdom, Peter is symbolically declaring that political power has been usurped by an illegitimate priesthood; by people whose right ears are unfit to be sprinkled with sacrificial blood, a priesthood that should never have been inducted into power.

This is an odd passage, both out of kilter with the rest of the narrative, and displaying an aspect of the apostles behaviour which is out of character with the gospel's message, so that an allegorical interpretation along the lines we have suggested seems the only possible one. It may be the remnant of a longer, more explicit passage. It supports the idea of a more active process of reform than merely gaining influence over the priesthood. As do the names of two of Jesus's disciples:

During the first half of the first century, as the Roman occupation of Israel hardened, the country began to divide into factions. When Jesus was about ten-years old a band of revolutionaries under the leadership of Judah the Galilean instituted a revolt against the census, forming themselves into a political band named the Zealots. [230] Following the fall of Jerusalem, the Zealots staged a four year long resistance in the desert stronghold of Masada. The Romans besieged their isolated fortress, year in, year out. When all hope was lost the Zealots committed suicide en mass. One of Jesus's disciples was known as Simon the Zealot, indicating his association with them.

Another revolutionary faction was known as the Sicarii. Their name probably comes from the short Roman dagger that they wielded, the *sica*. The Sicarii were responsible for many revolutionary acts, including the kidnap and holding to ransom of several of their own people, often culminating in murder when their demands were not met. The Sadducean high priest Jonathan was one of their victims. Judas Iscariot is simply a Hellenised version of the name Judas the Sicarian.

Thus two of the twelve apostles had names identifying them as members of political, revolutionary groups. This was no coincidence. But revolutionary allusions are not confined to the names and deeds of the apostles. One speech that Jesus makes is uncompromisingly aggressive in tone:

> *Do not think that I came to bring peace on earth. I did not come to bring peace but a sword. For I have come to set a man against his father, a daughter against her mother, and a daughter-in-law against her mother-in-law; and a man's enemies will be those of his own household.*[231]

There are also more subtle allusions in Jesus's speeches that suggest revolutionary aspirations:

> *The Jews answered and said to him, 'What sign do you show to us, since you do these things?' Jesus answered and said to them, 'Destroy this Temple, and in three days I will raise it up.' Then the Jews said, 'It has taken forty-six years to build this Temple, and will you raise it up in three days?' But he was speaking of the Temple of his body.*[232]

The last sentence, referring to the Temple of his body sounds like an afterthought. Might the original assertion, 'Destroy this Temple and in three days I will raise it up' be a revolutionary declaration thrown down as a gauntlet? When the accusation is repeated to Jesus by the high priest, he says nothing:

> *But at last two witnesses came forward and said, 'This fellow said, "I am able to destroy the Temple of God and to build it in three days."' And the high priest arose and said to him, 'Do you answer nothing? What is it these men testify against you?' But Jesus kept silent.* [233]

An even odder occurrence is reported at the moment of Jesus's death.

Jesus, when he had cried again with a loud voice, yielded up the ghost. And, behold, the veil of the Temple was rent in twain from the top to the bottom; and the earth did quake, and the rocks rent; [234]

The earthquake is relatively understandable; to the believer Jesus's death was a cosmic event and one might expect dramatic upheavals on this scale. The Jewish Bible describes the revelation on Mount Sinai in similarly dramatic terms. But what of the Temple veil? This refers to the curtain that divided off the most sacred part of the Temple, the holy of holies, into which only the high priest was allowed, and then only once a year, on the Day of Atonement. According to Jewish accounts, when the Romans destroyed the Temple, Titus entered the holy of holies and ripped the veil with his sword. The gospels, which in all likelihood post-date the Temple's destruction would have been written with an awareness of this incident. So unless the veil was ripped twice, once at Jesus's death and once at the Temple's destruction, which seems unlikely, the gospel authors must either be talking metaphorically or simply alluding to Titus's actions. The cruci-fixion of Jesus brought about the destruction of the Temple. The rhetoric that the gospels seem to be advancing is, had the early Christians been allowed to reform the Temple in the way that they wished, would the Romans have destroyed it and would the Jewish people have gone into spiritual exile?

A critical factor in planning any sort of upheaval in Temple life would have been the selection of the right candidate as high priest. He needed of course to be a member of the priestly caste, a descendant of the ancient high priest, Zadok, himself a descendant of Aaron. But more than this, he needed to be someone who could ensure the success of the reformation. A leader who projected authority, with a popular approach, capable of winning the support and affection of the masses. Within Jesus's circle one man immediately stood out. The gospels identify him for us.

There was in the days of Herod, the king of Judea, a certain priest named Zacharias ... His wife was of the daughters of Aaron, and her name was Elizabeth ... they had no child, because Elizabeth was barren, and they were both well advanced in years ... Then an angel of the Lord said to him ... your wife Elizabeth will bear you a son, and you shall call his name John ... he will be great in the sight of the Lord, and shall drink neither wine nor strong drink. He will also be filled with the Holy Spirit, even from his mother's womb.[235]

John the Baptist was both a charismatic preacher and a priest. A cousin of Jesus, he had already commenced his mission of baptism before Jesus began preaching. Baptism refers to a Jewish purification ritual, and immersing one's body wholly in running water, or man-made pools of a prescribed size and construction, was a necessary precondition for certain religious rites, including entry into the Temple.

The opening verses of the Gospel of Luke which deal with the annunciation of his birth, emphasise John's priestly heritage and compare him to Elijah, the herald of the messiah:

And he will go on before the Lord, in the spirit and power of Elijah, to turn the hearts of the fathers to their children and the disobedient to the wisdom of the righteous – to make ready a people prepared for the Lord.[236]

The story about John's birth is similar to the earlier story in the Jewish Bible about Samson's birth:

An angel appears to Samson's mother and tells her that she will have a son. He then gives the same message to Samson's father. The angel instructs them that Samson is to be a Nazirite. This means that he must abstain from alcohol, and neither cut his hair nor come into contact with any object or person which is ritually unclean. Similarly, John's parents are commanded not to allow him to drink alcohol. [237] His food is locusts – often understood to be locust beans, the fruit of the carob tree which grows profusely in Israel – and wild honey. [238] This suggests that he refrained from meat in order not to come into contact with food that may have been ritually unclean. The act of baptism, which John performed on those who came to him, is a cleansing ritual; anyone who became ritually unclean was obliged to baptise themselves fully in a river or ritual bath.

Samson's downfall comes about when the woman he loves cuts off his hair. John's death comes about when the woman his captor loves cuts off his head.

Both John and Samson are described in the Bible as being moved by the Holy Spirit. Jesus declares that John is the greatest of all people. John, however, is unexpectedly executed by Herod and his career is cut short in its prime. The account of his arrest, imprisonment, and execution occupies just eight verses in the longest version, chapter 14 of Matthew. Luke merely alludes to it and Mark recounts the events only to explain Herod's astonishment at the report that John has been raised from the dead. Neither the name of Herod's daughter, Salome, nor her dance of the seven veils, which was so strikingly portrayed in Christian and renaissance art, occur in any account; in fact it is the first-century Jewish historian Josephus who gives us her name. When reading the abrupt narrative of John's demise one gets the sense that this is an anti-climax which the gospel writers were unable to come to terms with.

Had the popular, charismatic, independently minded John been acclaimed and anointed as high priest in a reformed Temple, this would have led to a root and branch reform of the entire priestly establishment. It would have given early Christianity a political and religious power base that would have made it unstoppable in its ambitions to refashion the Jewish world. But his premature death made that impossible.

Jesus and his followers are not at this stage seeking to establish a new religion. They wish to reform the Jewish religious establishment. Central to this is the need to appoint a priestly dynasty, in which priests would regain their former role as the teachers and educators, faithful to Jesus's teachings, communicating them to a devout populace. The Holy Grail, Jesus's garment which asserts his right to inaugurate the new priesthood becomes the physical emblem of the reformation.

But before the early Christians could fully develop or establish their priestly aspirations, they were unexpectedly assisted by events. Little more than thirty years after the crucifixion, the Temple was destroyed and the priesthood neutered. By the time Paul came along there were no high priests to contend against, and there was no need for a Temple revolution to change the senior priesthood. The priests had ceased to be an obstacle; by destroying the Temple, God had not only taken all remaining power from them, he had removed any possibility that they could be a conduit for transmitting Jesus's teachings to the masses. All Paul had to do now was to explain that the reason that God had brought about their downfall was in order to return the priesthood to its rightful possessors; to the order of Melchizedek. This was an order which was not constrained by descent from Aaron and to which Jesus himself could legitimately lay claim; no longer as one who appoints priests, as Moses had done, but as the high priest himself.

The evidence that Jesus and his followers had some sort of reformist or revolutionary design on the Temple is strong; but it clashes severely with Paul's theology in which the Jewish Temple is a parochial irrelevance, whilst the true eternal priesthood belongs to Jesus himself. Which may explain why we can only find scattered allusions in the gospels to the revolutionary scheme. The death of John the Baptist and the subsequent destruction of the Jerusalem Temple itself made the intended revolution obsolete. It was written out of church history.

Yet, despite Paul's transformation of Jesus into a high priest, the Gospel of John somehow managed to preserve critical, early evidence to show that originally Jesus intended to install others into this role, to appoint new priests himself. And this evidence revolves around John's description of the Holy Grail. Which gives Paul a bit of a problem.

11

Paul's Problem

Paul was able to advance Christianity's ambitions and establish an agenda to become a world religion, precisely because the Jerusalem Temple had been destroyed[239]. Judaism was in an even deeper crisis than it had been during Jesus's time and it was no longer necessary for Christianity merely to become a reformed Judaism. On the contrary, Pauline doctrine now required the Jews to be converted to Christianity in order to bring about Jesus's second coming. Rather than struggling to spread Christianity directly to the recalcitrant Pharisaic Jews, it made strategic sense to first export the new religion to a much larger and more receptive audience, one which already existed within the Roman empire, from where it would in time feed back to the Jews. Quite accidentally, the Holy Grail was the only object that stood in Paul's way.

The biblical Epistle of Paul to the Hebrews is centred on the question of priesthood. As the title of the book suggests it was a letter written by Paul or one of his followers to a Hebrew community to persuade them of the validity of Christianity, in order that they would convert. In all probability this community was not originally Jewish, that is to say they were not descended from Jews. They belonged to a vast network of 'semi-Jews', people who had accepted the basic Jewish principles of monotheism without having fully converted to Judaism.

The Jewish idea of monotheism, the belief in one God, had spread through the Roman empire during the 1st century. Roman religion was still based on primitive myths and idol worship, but as the empire came into contact with the more sophisticated ideas prevalent in the near east, its population became attracted to new forms of religious expression. Jewish monotheism, the belief in one, all-powerful God, seemed to be an intellectually respectable position for sophisticated Romans to hold, even though the legal restrictions of Jewish life were less attractive.

It appears that the consequence of this cross-fertilisation of cultures was that monotheistic, quasi-Jewish communities established themselves. We know about them from Paul's writings and from Jewish and Roman sources. The Jews called them *yirei shamayim*, fearers of heaven, and it has been estimated that at one point one fifth of the western Roman empire subscribed to a Jewish-style monotheism.[240] These communities were where Christian missionary activity really took root, and were the breeding ground from which Roman Christianity emerged. They had already accepted monotheism but did not like the legalism of strict Judaism. When Paul came along with monotheistic Christianity, coupled with his assertions that the old law of the Jews had now been annulled, he found a willing and ready audience. Indeed it is clear from Paul's various epistles that his principal technique when spreading the message of Christianity was to demolish the validity of Pharisaic Judaism. In other words Judaism was already so well ingrained in these communities that all Paul had to do was to present a new, improved version to win their allegiance.

The annulment of the Law of Moses, or Torah, in favour of the belief in Jesus lies at the core of Paul's message:

A man is not justified by the works of the Torah but by faith in Jesus Christ.[241]

What purpose then does the Torah serve? It was added because of transgressions, till the seed should come to whom the promise was made; and it was appointed through angels by the hand of a mediator.[242]

For on the one hand there is an annulling of the former commandment because of its weakness and unprofitableness, for the

Torah made nothing perfect; on the other hand, there is the bringing in of a better hope, through which we draw near to God. [243]

In that he says, 'A new covenant', he has made the first obsolete. Now what is becoming obsolete and growing old is ready to vanish away. [244]

This is very different from Matthew's message:

Do not think that I came to destroy the Law or the Prophets. I did not come to destroy but to fulfil. [245]

So Paul is seeking to convert the Jews, and to annul their cultural heritage. A much bigger challenge than the Evangelists set for themselves; they were happy for Jesus, the Temple reformer, to build upon the heritage of the past. The Pauline argument, with which he attempts to persuade the Jews to accept his theology can be found in the Epistle to the Hebrews.

The Epistle to the Hebrews

The argument in Paul's letter to the Hebrews is based on Psalm 110:

The Lord said to my lord, 'Sit at My right hand' ... The Lord has sworn and will not repent, 'you are a priest forever, of the order of Melchizedek.' [246]

In the epistle Paul explains that in this verse, 'The Lord' is God and 'my lord' is Jesus. God places Jesus at his right hand and declares him to be an eternal priest, of the same priestly order as Melchizedek. Melchizedek is a little known figure from the Jewish Bible whom we encountered when we discussed Adam's clothes. He is a contemporary of Abraham, and described in Genesis as a priest of the most high God. In rabbinic legend Mechizedek is one of the names of Noah's son Shem; and in

Genesis, Abraham pays tithes to Melchizedek, in acknowledgement of his priesthood. Melchizedek, in return blesses Abraham.

> *Then Melchizedek king of Shalem brought out bread and wine; he was a priest of the most high God. And he blessed him and said: 'Blessed be Abraham of God most high, possessor of heaven and earth; And blessed be God most high, who has delivered your enemies into your hand.' And he gave him a tithe of all.*[247]

Paul's argument is that Jesus is heir to Melchizedek's priesthood; for if Melchizedek blesses Abraham, then he must be superior to him. Although Abraham's descendants, the Levites, eventually become the Jewish priests, Melchizedek had already occupied a higher spiritual level, or order. The Jewish priesthood was imperfect, Melchizedek's was perfect. Thus, when God tells Jesus that he is a priest, according to the order of Melchizedek, he is telling him that the earlier, superior priesthood has been restored, and the lesser Jewish priesthood has been annulled.

> *Therefore, if the ideal was to have the Levitical priesthood, under which the people received the Torah, what further need was there that another priest should rise from the order of Melchizedek, rather than the order of Aaron? When the priesthood is changed, there is also a necessary change of the Torah. For he of whom these things are spoken belongs to another tribe, from which no man has officiated at the altar. For it is evident that our lord arose from Judah, of which tribe Moses spoke nothing concerning priesthood ... And whereas they [the Jewish priests] became priests without an oath, he [Jesus] was not made priest without an oath, but with an oath, from He who said to him, The Lord has sworn and will not repent, 'you are a priest forever, according to the order of Melchizedek.'*[248]

According to Paul, Jesus's new, eternal priesthood is granted legitimacy by God's oath, a validation never given to the old Levitical priesthood descendants of Aaron. The key to it all is the phrase in Psalm 110,1: 'The Lord has sworn and will not repent, you are a priest forever, after the order of Melchizedek.'

> *Therefore, since we have a great high priest who has passed through the heavens, Jesus the son of God, let us hold fast our confession. For we do not have a high priest who cannot sympathize with our weaknesses, but one who has been tempted in all things as we are, yet without sin. Therefore let us draw near with confidence to the throne of grace, so that we may receive mercy and find grace to help in time of need.*[249]

The Jews of course saw things differently. Psalm 110 was not an invitation to Jesus to sit at God's right hand, but was an invitation to Abraham, who is called 'my lord' in Genesis 23,11. The words 'you are a priest forever after the order of Melchizedek' are based on a misunderstanding. The Hebrew phrase על דברתי actually means 'on account of the matter of', not 'after the order of'. The full translation of the Hebrew verse, according to the Jewish view, is: 'You are a priest forever, on account of the matter of Melchizedek'. Why? Because Melchizedek showed disrespect to God by blessing Abraham first. As a result he was divested of his priesthood, and it was diverted *eternally* to Abraham and his descendants, the Levites.

> *Rabbi Ishmael taught: God wanted the priesthood to descend from Shem*[250] *as it is said 'Then Melchizedek king of Salem brought out bread and wine; he was the priest of the most high God.'*[251] *When he blessed Abraham before he blessed God, Abraham said to him 'should one bless the servant before the master?' God removed the priesthood from him and gave it to Abraham, as it is said: God said to my lord....you are a priest forever, on account of the matter of Melchizedek.*[252]

The argument advanced by Paul, and the rabbinic text which is a response to Paul are the remaining literary fragments of what was once a hotly debated topic. It was still being argued over a thousand years later, resurfacing in Barcelona in 1263 when the great rabbinic scholar Moses ben Nahman, known as Ramban was commanded by King James I of Aragonia to defend Judaism against the charges of a Jewish apostate Pablo Christiani. Christiani presented a series of arguments to Ramban, each of which was designed to prove the superiority of Christianity over Judaism. Christiani's final argument was the one we have outlined above. Having heard Ramban's counter argument the king dismisses Christiani, declares the disputation ended and visits the synagogue the following week.

Paul's Christianity became the mainstream, but as with all movements, it started off as just one of several competing tendencies, most of which eventually fell by the wayside. In the end Paul's Christianity emerged out of the ashes of the Temple. The gospels came from a pre-destruction Israel, a nation in which although the priests still possessed religious authority, they were a corrupt establishment, one which even the Jews themselves, through the pharisaic rabbis, were trying to democratise. Paul's new theology claimed that Jesus himself had been appointed as a priest. That he was not from the priestly tribe of Levi did not matter,

For it is evident that our lord arose from Judah, of which tribe Moses spoke nothing concerning priesthood.[253]

The early Christians however knew nothing of such a claim. Their need was different. They knew full well that Jesus could not be a priest; he came from the royal family of David, not from the priestly family of Aaron. But they wanted to reform the religious establishment. Just as the Pharisees did. The tactic of the Pharisees was to establish a mass, popular movement, through education. To effect change from the outside.

Circumstances however forced the early Christians to chose a different strategy. They decided upon change from within. The Romans were in occupation of the land of Israel but for most of the time the Jews still had religious autonomy. To have a significant and enduring impact the emerging Christian movement sought to get themselves into a position of influence within the Jewish religious establishment. But they could only do so by exerting influence upon those institutions at the centre of power to which they could still gain access. Not upon those that the Pharisees already controlled.

Jesus's attempt to inaugurate a Temple revolution was no small matter and its significance cannot be over-emphasised. It is impossible to imagine how Christianity could have come into existence, had the revolt succeeded, because far from considering himself to be the founder of a new faith, the historical Jesus was in fact a political-religious leader with strong reformist tendencies. He wanted to reform the existing religious establishment to bring it in line with his ideals, seeking a new Israel and a recast Judaism that matched his values; one which had shaken itself free of the demoralising, oppressive influence of the Roman occupation, and of the stranglehold that they exerted over the priests who ministered in the Temple.

To achieve his reformist aims Jesus could either adopt an approach similar to that of the Pharisees, who were democratising Judaism through education, creating a new religious structure in which influence and leadership were the consequence of a person's learning and knowledge, rather than priestly birth; or he could aim to exert his personal influence over a priesthood that he and his followers had restored to its former glories, liberating it from its Roman masters, and regaining the affection of the masses for the institution, thereby overcoming the popularity of his Pharisee rivals.

Jesus chose the latter route, intending to bring the Temple

under his influence, by appointing a new hierarchy of priests who were drawn from his followers, and who were not stooges of the Roman occupation. The Holy Grail; the spiritual garment that symbolised Adam's clothes; the white, unstitched robe that Moses wore to inaugurate Aaron and his sons as the first priests, was the visible and deliberate symbol of this mission. If Jesus saw himself as a messiah, it was only because this title was applied to anyone who sought to free Israel from Roman dominance. He certainly didn't consider himself to be divine, or the son of God.

But this clearly thought out, deliberately constructed political agenda constituted Paul's problem. The Jesus that Paul was promoting was God himself; God who had assumed the guise of man. The Jesus of history however was a social and religious reformer. This latter dressed himself in clothes that signified religious authority, clothes that the people would be familiar with from their folklore. He dressed as Moses had dressed, to compare himself with him, and to appoint his own religious establishment. The garment was obtained from a legendary meeting with Moses and Elijah, the great national-religious leaders of Israel. So exalted was it in the public imagination, connected as it was with the garments of Adam, that John tells us the soldiers drew lots to see who would own it. It was not a garment that made a man a god, but it did set the wearer apart within human society, as a leader of men. It was the garment a leader put on to symbolise authority, to invest his successors. It was Adam's garment, and Adam was a man, not a god.

We know that Paul's theology was controversial, because it was not universally accepted. There were other sects, which fell by the wayside, who rejected Paul, and who appear to have adopted a religious outlook similar to that of the early Christians, certainly in terms of their relation to Judaism and the Jerusalem Temple. Chief amongst these were the Ebionites.

The word Ebionite comes from the Hebrew word meaning 'poor'. Their name suggests that they were a sect who kept their material possessions to a minimum, true to the frugal Christian ideal, an asceticism adopted by many monastic orders in subsequent centuries. Unfortunately little information about the Ebionites has survived. Nearly all that we do know is contained in the writings of Ireneaus, Bishop of Lyons, which date from around 175 CE.

> *Those who are called Ebionites ... use the gospel according to Matthew only, and repudiate the apostle Paul, maintaining that he was an apostate from the law. As to the prophetical writings,* [254] *they endeavour to expound them in a somewhat singular manner: they practise circumcision, persevere in the observance of those customs which are enjoined by the Torah, and are so Judaic in their style of life, that they even adore Jerusalem as if it were the house of God.*

Ireneaus considered that the Ebionites adored Jerusalem as if it were the house of God. The house of God was the very phrase that the Jewish writings used to describe the Temple. [255] According to the Gospel of Luke, the last words which Jesus speaks to his disciples, when he appears to them after the resurrection were:

> *Behold, I send the Promise of My Father upon you; but tarry in the city of Jerusalem until you are imbued with power from on high*[256].

The climax of the Gospel of Luke is an instruction to his disciples to remain in Jerusalem, which is in line with the Ebionite perspective. The forgotten history of the Ebionites would undoubtedly paint a different picture of Jesus and early Christianity than is commonly accepted. [257]

The clothing for which the soldiers cast lots, the *goral*, has taken on a sacred character, becoming the holy goral, or as we know it, the Holy Grail. Yet the only reference to it in the entire

Christian Bible is in John 19,23.

The Holy Grail establishes Jesus's right to install a new priesthood, confirming the evidence in the Christian Bible that he wished to at the least reform the Temple, perhaps even to instigate a fully-fledged revolution if such proved necessary, in order to reform Judaism in line with his religious approach. The Holy Grail placed Jesus on a par with Moses. It did not however elevate him above Moses and proclaim his divinity, and in many ways it limits Jesus's status. It suggests that he and his followers saw him as a Jewish reformer, but not as the founder of a new religion, and certainly not as a divine messiah. First the death of John the Baptist, then the crucifixion of Jesus, however, put an end to all the plans for Temple reform. Jesus's passing represented the end of the reformist dream. The early Christians preserved his teachings, but in the absence of their founder and no longer with any national influence, their aspirations were denied.

The Holy Grail passed on Jesus's death to a Roman soldier, an unknown man, beyond the control of the disciples.

In time things turned out well for Christianity. In a separate development the Romans destroyed the Temple, thereby plunging the Jewish religion into crisis, Paul was able to provide a far more determined, wholly inspirational theological foundation for Christianity that allowed it to emerge as a beacon of hope within a defeated nation. But the Holy Grail remained as a symbol of an early, less ambitious movement. The unstitched robe, were its true significance to be disclosed, would not just have been an embarrassment; its existence would have undermined all of Paul's work, and that of his successors.

If the Pauline church were to encourage attention to focus on this unstitched robe, the Holy Grail, they would in effect be acknowledging Jesus's status as another great Jewish leader in a succession of great leaders; and by implication they would be denying his most important quality, the thing that set him apart from ordinary mortals, his divinity.

Paul therefore could not countenance a situation in which Jesus was perceived as merely the instigator of a Temple revolution, in which he appointed others to function as priests. To overcome any suggestion of this he declared that Jesus was himself a priest, setting out his justification of this in the place where it would have the most impact, his Epistle to the Hebrews.

Of course Paul struggles to prove his point in the Epistle because Jesus was a descendant of King David, and in Israelite society, one could not be both a king and a priest. But it is essential for Paul to prove his point, in order to refute the evidence of the grail, that Jesus was a priest-maker and not a priest.

Meanwhile, mention of the unstitched robe remained in the Gospel of John. It is possible that it had been excised from the synoptic gospels precisely because it conflicts with Paul's theology, which is why they speak of the soldiers drawing lots over all of Jesus's garments, not just the unstitched robe. But it remained in John's more individualistic work, in the one gospel that differed significantly in style, content and character. Which might in itself tell us something of the history and transmission of John's gospel- did the Pauline school ever gain influence over those who guarded its editorial integrity? Nevertheless, because it remained in John, it needed to be dealt with. [258]

And so we find that the unstitched robe of John's gospel, no longer acknowledged as the Holy Grail, was invested with a religious significance of its own. One which still carried political and pragmatic undertones, but that were related to the emerging Christian church itself, and no longer to the Jewish religion of Jesus's time.

12

What Happened to the Holy Grail?

Having disposed of the notion of Jesus as priest-maker, Pauline Christianity had to respond to the Holy Grail, which as a central symbol in the crucifixion narrative was in danger of acquiring iconic status. The Holy Grail could not just be forgotten but it could be allegorised.

Between 248 and 258 CE Thacius Caecilius Cyprianus, known as Cyprian, was Bishop of Carthage, near the modern city of Tunis in north Africa. This was the time of the Decian persecutions, when the early church was being mercilessly victimised by the Romans. Cyprian himself went into in hiding and many Christians became apostates, publicly worshipping Roman gods, often purchasing certificates which testified that they had done so. But once the persecutions began to wane, these apostate Christians attempted to re-enter the church from which they had disassociated themselves.

A group of five Christian priests, headed by Novatus, believing that all souls had the right to redemption and should be given a second chance, began to readmit the lapsed Christians. They did this without reference to the bishops of the church, who opposed the practice, and re-admitted the apostates in such a way that the bishops found themselves faced with a fait accompli. Cyprian feared that as a result of such behaviour anarchy was knocking on the door of the emerging church. He believed that it was essential for the future survival of the ecclesiastical body that authority and discipline be restored. And so he wrote his celebrated pamphlet, *De Ecclesiae Catholicae Unitate*, On the Unity of the Catholic Church and used the unstitched robe as the symbol of the Church's unity.

Whoever stands aloof from the Church ... is cut off from the promises given to the Church; and he that leaves the Church of Christ attains not to Christ's rewards. He is an alien, an enemy. He who will not have the Church for his mother, cannot have God for his father ... This sacrament of unity, this bond of peace inseparable and indivisible, is indicated when in the Gospel the robe of the Lord Jesus Christ was not divided at all or rent ... Divine Scripture says, 'But as for the robe, since it was unstitched, woven throughout, from the part above, they said among themselves: "Let us not rend it, but cast lots for it to see whose it shall be."' That garment stood for the unity which comes 'from the part above', that is, from heaven and from the Father, a unity which could not be rent at all by him that received it and had it in possession; he took it indivisibly in its unbreakable entirety. He who rends and divides the Church of Christ cannot possess the clothing of Christ ...[259]

At a time when the internal cohesion of the church was in danger of being undermined, Cyprian deliberately introduced the indivisible seamless robe as a symbol of the essential, inseparable nature of the faith and its institutions. So in an ironic twist, the unstitched robe itself undergoes a transfiguration. From a symbol of revolution and division within the Jewish religious establishment, to a symbol of unity of the church.

About sixty years after Cyprian, a theological dispute arose in the church over the relationship between Jesus and God. The traditional view of the church, developed by Paul, was that Jesus was the Son of God, and was in every way divine. The opposing view, initiated by Arius, and known as Arianism, regarded Jesus as a lesser divinity, a demi-god. This position was heavily influenced by Gnosticism, which in some manifestations subscribed to a dualist view of two gods in competition with each other. Arius's great ideological opponent was Peter, Bishop of Alexandria. In the apocryphal work, Genuine Acts of Peter, which claims to present a history of his life, the following passage appears:

> *The hidden treachery of Arius surpasses all iniquity and impiety,*
> *and not asserting this of mine own self, have I sanctioned his excom-*
> *munication. For in this night, whilst I was solemnly pouring forth*
> *my prayers to God, there stood by me a boy of about twelve years,*
> *the brightness of whose face I could not endure, for this whole cell in*
> *which we stand was radiant with a great light. He was clothed with*
> *a linen tunic divided into two parts, from the neck to the feet, and*
> *holding in his two hands the rents of the tunic, he applied them to*
> *his breast to cover his nudity. At this vision I was stupefied with*
> *astonishment. And when boldness of speech was given to me, I*
> *exclaimed: Lord, who hath rent thy tunic? Then said he, Arius hath*
> *rent it, and by all means beware of receiving him into communion;*
> *behold, to-morrow they will come to entreat you for him. See,*
> *therefore, that thou be not persuaded to acquiesce.*[260]

Peter's vision of Jesus with his seamless robe torn asunder is based upon Cyprian's idea that the unstitched robe represents the unanimity of the church. The robe becomes the means whereby Jesus himself, here in the guise of a twelve year old boy, demands of his followers that unity and authority are restored. By the third century the transformation of the garment from John's original Holy Grail, associated with revolution at the heart of the Jewish religion, to a symbol of the unity of the Christian church, is complete.

First Cyprian then Peter recast the unstitched robe in a manner which removed any suggestion that it was an essential part of either a Temple reformation, or the introduction of a new order of Jewish priests. By doing so they overlook the question of why a garment that symbolised church unity should be awarded by lottery to those people who crucified its founder and intended to expunge his memory from history. If the garment symbolised the eternal church, rather than a temporal political-religious ambition, why do we not hear how the apostles reacted to its confiscation? We would have expected them to try to reclaim it. That would be the least they could do, if it was of such profound significance.

Cyprian's position is unconvincing. It is as if he is using the metaphor of church unity to deflect attention from the obvious association of this garment with Jewish reformation. Indeed, it appears that the reason that the garment becomes associated with the unity of the church is an ingenious attempt to conceal the revolutionary significance of the robe. Which was to instigate change in the Jewish world by seeking to restore religious influence to a newly reformed priesthood, pitting them against a Pharisaic opposition whose own reformist agenda was based on the advancement of a democratic meritocracy.

As for the Holy Grail as originally conceived, apart from the obscure references in the gospels to a garment or garments that the soldiers divided by lottery, hardly a trace remained in early Christian literature or belief. Had it not been for a Christian society that venerated relics and a Jewish world that never threw a holy item away, we may never have heard of it.

But the grail was not destroyed. It could not have been. This was a society that treated sacred objects with utmost care. The ethos prevails in strict Jewish circles even today. In the world into which Jesus and the apostles had been born, sacred items, whether written texts, utensils or garments are not thrown away. They are buried and allowed to decompose naturally.

Reverent disposal of holy objects has been going on for millennia. In the course of the past hundred and twenty years, three major finds have been uncovered that illustrate this. These finds have not only taught us much about life in ancient Israel, they prove that as long ago as Jesus's time, holy objects such as the Holy Grail were carefully preserved even when they were no longer usable.

In 1898 two English travellers, Mrs Gibson and Mrs Lewis

purchased a Hebrew document in Egypt. Intrigued, they showed it to Dr Solomon Shechter, Reader in Rabbinics at Cambridge University. He guessed, correctly, that it had come from a depository of obsolete documents in the old synagogue at Fostat, near Cairo. He organised an expedition to the synagogue and discovered a false wall, behind which was a cavity known as Genizah, or storage-place. Shechter assembled a team to clear out the Genizah. They found that for over a thousand years Jews had been depositing their worn out bibles, prayer books and sacred texts behind this wall, as well as many documents of ordinary life which were no longer needed. Because holy objects, and even day-to-day documents written in the sacred tongue, were never thrown away.

In 1945 an Arab worker digging near the town of Nag Hammadi in Upper Egypt came across a large earthenware urn. In it were previously unknown papyrus books that have since been dated to the year 390. These books turned out to be gospels sacred to a sect of gnostic Christians, the most challenging of all the opponents of what was to become established Christianity. The discovery of these documents has fundamentally changed scholars' understanding of the relationship between Gnosticism and the early Christian church. In all probability the documents were buried to keep them from the authorities, or from an ideological opponent. They were buried, not destroyed, because this was the accepted way to treat holy objects. Their sanctity was such that they could not be destroyed.

The Dead Sea scrolls, the first of which were accidentally found in the remote desert hillside on the western cliffs of the world's lowest natural lake in 1947, led to a search which uncovered thousands of fragments of scrolls in eleven caves. The scrolls provided evidence about the life of the priestly Qumran ascetic sect during the final centuries of the pre-Christian era. They contain important textual information about the Bible, present a mystical, heavenly-based view of priestly Judaism far removed from anything that Jesus or the Pharisees were teaching and include many previously unknown books and documents. They have revolutionised our understanding of life in ancient Israel, of the Bible and of Jewish social and religious development. Like the Nag Hammadi documents, the Dead Sea Scrolls were stored in pottery casks. They were preserved in this way because holy objects were never destroyed.

Although the account in the Talmud indicates that the Holy Grail was once in the hands of the Roman enemies of Christianity, we can be sure that even if they had not got their hands on it sooner, by the fifth century, when the church became the official religion of Rome, it would have reclaimed the mysterious, dangerous unstitched robe.

The Legends

So what happened to the Holy Grail, after we last hear of it in Rome? What happened to this garment that has spawned a thousand legends, that captured the imagination of myriads of questers and enthusiasts, from at least the eleventh century down to our own day?

The quest for the grail first described by Chretien de Troyes, and developed in the later Arthurian literature was based on the false assumption that the grail was a chalice. At the same time, possession of the unstitched robe was claimed by at least two religious centres neither of which knew, or at least did not admit to the fact that it was the Holy Grail.

In the middle ages every religious building of any significance claimed to have relics, of saints, evangelists, and even of Jesus himself. Relics turned a religious site from merely a place to pray into a centre of pilgrimage. The faithful would flock to pay homage before a relic, in the belief that it would bring salvation. Thousands of relics were claimed, the vast majority of which subsequently turned out to be forgeries. Even today there is controversy over the authenticity of the most famous of all, the

Turin Shroud; the cloth in which Jesus's body is supposed to have been wrapped. The earliest post-biblical mention of relics in Christianity is in a work called the Martyrdom of Polycarp. Polycarp who was bishop of Smyrna, was put to death in 155 CE. In the account of his death, his followers tell us:

We took up his bones, which are more valuable than precious stones and finer than refined gold, and laid them in a suitable place, where the Lord will permit us to gather ourselves together, as we are able, in gladness and joy and to celebrate the birthday of his martyrdom.[261]

The 4th century church father, Jerome, ruled that relics could not be worshipped, but could be venerated:

We do not worship, we do not adore, for fear that we should bow down to the creature rather than to the creator, but we venerate the relics of the martyrs in order to adore him better ...[262]

Several relics of Jesus are claimed to exist. These include pieces of the cross, his baby blanket, the loincloth that he wore on the cross (after the soldiers had divided his garments), and his foreskin. Medieval believers, caught up in a frenzy of relic hunting, included the unstitched robe on their wish list, and because, unlike most relics, this garment had been specifically mentioned in the Christian Bible, it assumed a significance and importance vastly superior to some of the other, more spurious souvenirs that were being hunted. By the 12th century the tunic was said to have been discovered, and several places laid claim to it. Most notably the priory in Argenteuil in France, and the cathedral of Trier in Germany.

There are two legends which claim to trace what happened to the seamless robe. Both are relatively late and cannot be claimed either as authentic, or to throw too much light on the true significance of this garment for Christianity. But however fanciful a legend or piece of folklore may be, it is often based on an earlier account, a kernel of folk memory, which may provide clues to the past.

One legend claims to explain the arrival of the seamless robe in the city of Trier. It occurs in a 12th century German poem, Orendel. In this poem, following the crucifixion Pilate gave the robe to a Jew who, unable to remove the blood stains, discarded it into the sea, where it was swallowed by a whale. Meanwhile Orendel, son of the king of Trier, had been shipwrecked near Palestine and was enslaved as a fisherman. He catches the whale, finds the robe and brings it back to Trier, before setting off to become king of Jerusalem.

The robe, swallowed by a whale, echoes the story of Jonah.

We have seen how lots were cast over both Jonah and the seamless robe, and now it appears that each is swallowed by a whale. Both Jesus and Jonah are restored after 3 days, Jonah spewed up by the whale, Jesus resurrected. In the Trier legend the robe seems to symbolise the resurrection, but it bears no relation either to the official role of the robe as a symbol of church unity, nor to its true significance as a political mantle of revolution.

The earlier, and more relevant legend occurs in a work entitled 'Death of Pilate'. Tiberius, emperor of Rome is sick and hears that there is a miracle worker named Jesus in Israel. He sends for him only to discover that Pilate has had him crucified. Furious, he summons Pilate to Rome. Pilate, in great fear puts on Jesus's seamless robe, which he has acquired from the soldiers who drew lots for it at the crucifixion. Tiberius sees the robe and against his will his anger softens; he finds he is unable to speak harshly to Pilate. But as soon as he sends Pilate away, his anger returns. Summoning Pilate again, he finds himself once more divested of his anger and speaking kindly to him. This pattern keeps repeating itself. After a while it dawns on Tiberius that

Pilate must be protected in some way. Told that he is wearing Jesus's unstitched tunic, he orders that Pilate be stripped of his robe and returned to his presence. This time his rage remains unassuaged and Tiberius is able to condemn Pilate to death.

This legend confirms the appearance of the seamless robe in Rome. In addition to the Talmudic tradition about Adam's garments and the lame man, which places the Holy Grail in the hands of the pagan rulers of Rome, we now have a Christian legend that claims the robe was taken there by Pilate, who presumably removed it from the possession of the soldier who had won it in the lottery.

It is possible that Jesus's followers themselves acquired back the mysterious garment from the lucky soldier, shortly after the crucifixion. And that they kept it safe for as long as they could, for nearly thirty-five years. Until the Romans destroyed the city of Jerusalem, looted everything within it, including all the Temple treasures, and carried off many of the population as slaves.

The arch of Titus, with its bas-relief depicting the sack of the Temple has been subjected to intense scrutiny over the years. Scholars are in little doubt that the Temple treasures depicted on the arch are genuine representations. The evidence from the arch is backed up by Josephus, the prominent Jewish-Roman historian of the first century. Josephus describes Titus's triumphant entry in Rome, carrying the Menorah, the golden table and copies of the Tablets of the Law, together with other, lesser spoils.

But for those that were taken in the Temple of Jerusalem, they made the greatest figure of them all; that is, the golden table, of the weight of many talents; the candlestick also, that was made of gold ... these lamps were seven in number, and represented the dignity of the number seven among the Jews; and carried last of all the spoils, was the Torah of the Jews. After these spoils passed by a great many men, carrying the images of Victory, whose structure was entirely either

of ivory or of gold. After which Vespasian marched in the first place,
and Titus followed him; Domitian also rode along with them, and
made a glorious appearance, and rode on a horse that was worthy of
admiration.[263]

The Holy Grail may have travelled to Rome on the same ship that carried the Temple treasures and may well have been carried into the city in the procession that Josephus describes.

On January 27, 1996 the *Jerusalem Post* reported that Israel's Minister Of Religious Affairs had met Pope John Paul II to ask him to help him locate Israel's ancient Menorah – the golden, seven branched candlestick which had stood in the Jewish Temple in Jerusalem until its destruction by the Romans in the year 70 CE.

On January 15th 2004, Associated Press reporter Gavin Rabinowitz reported that Israel's chief rabbis, who were due to meet the Pope, said they hoped to get permission to search Vatican storerooms for artefacts including the golden Menorah brought into Rome by the soldiers who had looted the Jerusalem Temple on that fateful day nearly 2,000 years ago.

Although the Vatican maintains a stony silence on the question of whether the Menorah is stored in its cavernous vaults, there is ample evidence that it was once taken to Rome. Along with many other sacred, Jewish Temple treasures and vessels.

Is the Holy Grail amongst them? To claim so would be highly speculative. But it is not beyond the bounds of possibility.

Whichever way the grail got to Rome, the last that we hear of it is in the Talmudic account of the ceremony of the healthy man riding upon the lame man. This ceremony could have taken place no later than the year 500 CE, when the Talmud was completed. In all probability it took place much earlier, since Christianity had been adopted as the official religion of Rome one hundred years before this, and clearly the legend relates to a period when Christianity was being persecuted by the Romans. After this all we hear is the legend of Tiberius and Pilate. Although there can be little doubt that, if the robe was indeed in Rome, it would have returned to the church when they achieved prominence, it remains most likely that in time the garment disintegrated and will never be found.

The Reality

But the greatest mystery of the Holy Grail quest is that nobody ever claimed to find it.

Of course we now know that it could not be found, because its seekers were looking for the wrong thing. A cup not a garment. They would not have known it if they had found it. But we also know that most claims made in the middle ages about religious relics were false; they were the products of an overzealous imagination on the part of the finder, or they were a fraudulent assertion made in the hope of selling the find for a fortune.

Why then, in a medieval church obsessed with relics, did nobody claim to have found the chalice that they were seeking, that they believed to be the grail? Many other speculative claims were made by people who professed to have a found a remnant of the cross or of other objects associated with Jesus's burial. Despite the continuous quest for the grail, which continues to our day, it appears that nobody has ever seriously claimed to possess it. Or if they have, it has not been brought to public attention.

One would have thought there was money and fame to be had in depositing an ancient chalice in a monastery somewhere, and claiming that it was that which Percival of the Round Table had seen in the castle of the Fisher King. Yet no one has ever done this. Indeed the quest for the Holy Grail seems to be an end in itself, to find it would be to annihilate it.

We don't know how the legend of the lost *goral* first surfaced after its initial concealment. We can however conceive that the secret of the robe had been imperfectly concealed, that once hints of the *goral* emerged and became part of the medieval story-tellers' repertoire, its true identity began to come clear to the learned monks and bishops. Perhaps they in turn feared, lest its discovery open a Pandora's box of troublesome secrets and contradictory theologies.

What better way then for the church to conceal the identity of the grail than to encourage its followers in their quest for the wrong thing? To encourage the belief that *goral* was the French word *graal*, to deflect its hunters from knowing its true identity, and to send them on a wild goose chase? The Holy Grail was too powerful a theological opponent for the church to do anything other than mask its existence altogether; if the Pauline theologians could have written it out of John's gospel in the same way that it may have been excised from the other three gospels, there is little doubt they would have done so.

The history of the Holy Grail offers us a remarkable insight into the theological problems of the early church. Unlike earlier religions Christianity did not evolve as part of a national culture or local society. Its basic beliefs did not develop from the myths and revelations handed down by former generations. Rather it was inspired by one man, and its mythology was carefully, artificially constructed in such a way as to echo the folklore of the society from which it emerged. This led at times to a conflict between historical fact and the theological agenda of the faith's architects. The Holy Grail is an outstanding example of this.

Having failed in his attempt to institute Temple reform, following the death of John the Baptist, Jesus pursued an even more ambitious mission to redeem the sins of his followers, one which required his death as a scapegoat. The lottery that took place at the crucifixion was a theologically essential element of a scapegoat sacrifice. But the garment which was used as the lot, or *goral*, happened to be both a politically dangerous symbol, as well as a mystical bond with the Adam of the Garden of Eden. As such it affirmed Jesus's role as a leader determined to reform the

Jerusalem Temple and therefore threatened to undermine the entire structure of Christianity.

Yet the unstitched robe could not be entirely written out of Christianity. So a new creation was devised, a Holy Grail that never existed, popularised in romance and legend, a cover up to deflect the inquisitive. One that could never be found and that would maintain its mystery until the end of time. As long as people did not enquire too deeply.

Notes

Notes to Chapter 1

1   The word synoptic in this sense derives from the Greek 'synopsis' meaning to give a general view, or to be viewed together. These synoptic gospels give an account of the events in the life of Jesus, communicated from a similar perspective, and presenting a similar point of view. They can be set out in three parallel columns and compared and contrasted.

2   Friedrich Nietzsche, The Antichrist 1895

3   We will use the phrase Old Testament for convenience but it is not a phrase that Jews are keen on since it suggests that their bible has been superseded by another.

4   The process whereby certain books were included in the Jewish Bible whilst others were excluded wasn't straight-forward. In part, the decision as to which books it would comprise was an organic one, and it is inconceivable that works such as the Five Books of Moses or many of the Psalms would not attain canonical status. They were the essence of the Jewish religion. But others were included as part of a process of deliberation, at a relatively late date. Jewish tradition attributes these deliberations to a group of religious leaders known as the Men of the Great Synagogue, who are alleged to have flourished between the fifth and second centuries BCE. There is however no independent or objective evidence to confirm either the existence of this group, or their editorial role. The closest we get to historical evidence comes from a few brief passages in the Talmud, the vast compendium of legal, ethical, and religious discussions which took place in rabbinic academies in Babylon and Israel between the third and fifth centuries CE. These passages imply that the Jewish Bible was not given its final

shape until a group of rabbis thrashed the matter out in Yavneh, a small town in the south-west of Israel, not far from the modern Tel Aviv, towards the end of the first century CE. According to the Talmud, the rabbis were concerned about the content of a few books, notably Ecclesiastes, Song of Songs, and Ezekiel, which contained elements that could be considered as contradictory to accepted Jewish belief. The fact that the Talmud tells us that these books were finally included in the second century CE indicates that the bulk of the Jewish Bible had already attained a stable state by this time, even though it was not known as a Bible.

5 This canon is probably that set out in the Decretum Gelasianum de libris recipiendis et non recipiendis, traditionally attributed to Gelasius, bishop of Rome 492-496 CE. The first definitive list of books in the New Testament is found in the Muratorian canon, a Greek text which dates from around the year 180 CE. Although there was never any debate after this date about the inclusion of the four gospels in the Christian Bible, other books were less readily accepted.

6 Matthew 26,51; Mark 14,47; Luke 22,50; John 18,26. In each version Jesus protests against the violence and in Luke he heals the servant's ear.

7 John 12, 7-8

8 This is a quote from Isaiah 56,7

9 Matthew 21,12-13. The 'den of thieves' quote is from Jeremiah 7,11

10 Bruce Chilton's assertion that Jesus's actions were designed to introduce a change in Jewish law to enable greater public access to sacrifices, is wrong. He compares Jesus's actions with those of Hillel described in Talmud Babli Betzah 20a and Shimon ben Gamliel in Mishnah Keritot 1.7. But in those cases a legal discussion was advanced, in Jesus's case the action seems to have been driven by zealotry, not legalism. Bruce Chilton; The Temple of Jesus, Pennsylvania State

University Press, 1992 pp. 101-2

11 Mishnah Demai 1,2

12 Mishnah Shekalim 7,2

13 Mechilta d'Rabbi Yishmael, Mas. d'Hodesh 10

14 Talmud Babli Sanhedrin 101b

15 Josephus: Wars 2:118; Antiquities 18:23.

16 Josephus: Antiquities 20:97

17 For a good summary of the tensions and conflicts during the period see Elias J. Bickerman, the Jews in the Greek age, particularly chapter 25, Faith and History, pp 288 ff.

18 Matthew 3, 1-6

19 Midrash Tanhuma (ed. Buber), Va'era 22

20 The leading figure of his generation.

21 Mishna Ta'anit 3,8

22 Talmud Berachot 33a

23 Talmud Ta'anit 34b

24 Talmud Yoma 53b

25 Mishna Avot 3,9

26 ibid

27 John 7, 14-23

28 Talmud, Sanhedrin 65b (all references to 'Talmud' refer to the Babylonian Talmud unless otherwise stated.)

29 Talmud, Shabbat 33b

30 Luke 2, 41-6

31 Matthew 21,23

Notes to Chapter 2

32 Jubilees is part of what is known as the Pseudepigrapha. These are books written in biblical style although they were clearly composed at a much later date. They were not included in either the Jewish or Christian bibles. Jubilees is what is known as a re-written Bible, adding details and legends to the narratives in the Jewish Bible and setting events in 50 year cycles, which correspond to the ancient

Jewish Jubilee year. Originally written in Hebrew, the earliest record of it that we know is in Ethiopic. It is considered to date from the first half of the first century BCE.

33 The first two of the four books of the Maccabees, which chronicle the history of the Greek occupation of Israel and the subsequent Jewish rebellion which ousted them are still published in the Apocrypha, accepted by many Christians as a semi-sacred appendix to the Bible.

34 The nineteenth century school of biblical criticism, of which the leading proponent was Julius Wellhausen, sought to place the bible on a scientific footing. Wellhausen claimed, inter alia, that the Pentateuch, the five books attributed to Moses, were in fact composed from four separate sources and not written by one man. In the Pentateuch Moses leads the Israelites towards the Promised Land but foretells their eventual exile from the selfsame territory. Wellhausen and subsequent biblical critics consider that this national myth was written down much later, long after both the settlement of the land of Israel and the subsequent exile of the Jews to Babylon in 586 BCE. In other words the Pentateuch contains mythical history, not prophecy.

35 Thought to be the Persian king Xerses I though earlier scholars identified him with Atarxerses I

36 Esther, 1,1

37 Matthew 26,1-2: When Jesus had finished saying all these things, he said to his disciples, "As you know, the Passover is two days away—and the son of man will be handed over to be crucified.". Parallels occur in chapter 14 of Mark and chapter 22 of Luke.

38 Matthew 21, 8-9

39 John 12,13

40 Although the Christian commemoration Palm Sunday falls in the week before Easter this is probably due to an error on the part of the later church fathers who did not recognise the

Jewish ritual significance of the palm branches.

41 Matthew 21, 1-7

42 Geza Vermes The Authentic Gospels of Jesus (London 2003). The misunderstanding of the Hebrew has come about, according to Vermes, due to a failure to recognise the literary parallelism in Zechariah 9,9.

43 Genesis 22 1- 19

44 Genesis 24,2

45 Genesis 14,14: 'And he prepared his disciple(s)', which Bereshit Rabbah identifies as Eliezer.

46 Numbers 22,22

47 Midrash Tanhuma Balak 8

48 Midrash Bereshit Rabbah 56,3

49 Matthew 16,24

50 Parallel accounts occur in Mark 8,24 and Luke 9,23.

51 John 1:36

52 John 1:29

53 Revelations 22,3

54 Bereshit Rabbah 56,4

55 The fact that this is a Greek pun attests both to the antiquity of this interpretation and to the ease with which the educated classes in ancient Israel could switch between languages. Greek had been known in Israel since at least the time of Alexander the Great, in the 4th Century BCE.

56 According to Jewish tradition Isaac was thirty seven years old at the time of the Akedah. It was theologically necessary for him to be fully grown in order that he could be considered an active, voluntary participant in the drama, and not an unwilling victim.

57 Genesis 22, 11-12

58 Genesis 22, 14-19

59 The full text can be found in Hebrew Verse, ed. & tr. T. 33 Carmi, Penguin 1981 p.379

60 Poem by Benjamin ben Zerach, mid 1th Century, recited as

part of the penitential prayers for the Fifth Day.

61 Poem by Isaac ben Reuben of Barcelona, mid 1th Century, recited as part of the penitential prayers for the Eve of the Day of Atonement.

62 2 Maccabees 7, 1-41

63 Augustine: De Civitate Dei 18,36

64 Lamentations Rabbah 1:53

Notes to Chapter 3

65 Babylonian Talmud Shabbat 89b

66 Shir HaShirim Rabbah 8:1

67 The evangelical website biblia.com lists a total of 121 prophecies about Jesus in the book of Isaiah, together with those passages in the New Testament where they are said to have been fulfilled.

68 Isaiah 53, 3-7

60 Lewis Carroll: Through the Looking Glass, 1872, Chapter 6

70 Isaiah 9, 4-6

71 ibid 11, 1-5

72 ibid 11, 6-10

73 Ezekiel chapter 34, also Jeremiah 23, 5-6

74 Talmud Yerushalmi Ta'anit 4,5 (68d)

75 A star will issue out of Jacob, and a ruler from Israel...

76 1 Kings 8,17

77 Matthew 1, 1-17

78 Luke 18, 31-3

79 Matthew 27,63, Mark 8,31; 9,31; 10,34

80 Matthew 15,32.

81 Luke 2, 41-6

82 Hosea 6,2

83 Matthew 12,40

84 Luke 1,27 and 1,34

85 Matthew 1,23

86 Shemot Rabbah 3,12

87 Bereshit Rabbah 63,25

88 Bereshit Rabbah 87

89 Exodus 20

90 Bereshit Rabbah 68,4

91 Daniel 2

92 Kohelet Rabbah 1,5

93 Genesis 6, 1-4

94 Genesis 4,1

95 Hosea 2, 21-22

96 Ezekiel 16 was forbidden to be read publicly in the synagogue because of its unpleasant language and its graphic portrayal of Israel as a swamp-sodden foundling (Mishnah Megillah 4,10)

97 Ezekiel 16, 8-34

98 Proverbs 8, 22-31

99 Wisdom of Solomon 7, 24- 8,3

100 Philo, On Cherubim, 44 (49)

101 Philo, On Drunkenness VIII (30)

102 WF Albright, "The Goddess of Life and Wisdom" <u>American Journal of Semitic Languages and Literature</u> 36 (1919-20) pp 258-294.

103 Bernhard Lang <u>Wisdom and the Book of Proverbs</u>

104 The literature is extensive. See particularly Philippe Borgeaud, <u>Mother of the Gods. From Cybele to the Virgin Mary</u>. Baltimore: The Johns Hopkins University Press, 2004.

Notes to Chapter 4

105 L. W. King, Chronicles Concerning Early Babylonian Kings, 105 II, London, 1907

106 Luke 16,6

107 Acts 13,39

108 Matthew 5,1

109 Matthew 8,1

110 Matthew 14, 23-25

111 Matthew 15, 29-30

112 Matthew 28,16

113 Exodus 3,1

114 Exodus chapters 19-20

115 Exodus chapters 32-35

116 Deuteronomy 34,1

117 Deuteronomy 9,9 and 9,19

118 Matthew 4,8

119 Babylonian Talmud Sanhedrin 101b

120 Matthew 2,16

121 Exodus 4,19

122 Matthew 2,20

Notes to Chapter 5

123 Matthew 17, 1-12. See also Luke 9, 28-36 and Mark 9, 2-13

124 Biblical scholars have recognised for years that different sections of the book of Isaiah were written by different authors. When we refer to Isaiah in this book we are speaking of the author(s) of chapters 40 onwards, commonly referred to as Deutero-Isaiah, which contain the bulk of the prophecies which Christianity associates with Jesus.

125 2 Kings, 2,11

126 Malachi 4,5

127 I Kings 19,19, Elijah appoints Elisha to be his successor by casting his mantle upon him.

128 Exodus chapters 19-20

129 Exodus 33,18-34,9

130 Exodus 34,29-35

131 Luke 9,33

132 Mark 9,6.

133 The word is סכה in Hebrew, pronounced sukkah

134 See Isaiah 1,8 for an example of parallelism that defines the word.

135 Leviticus 16, 10-22

136 John 3,17

137 John 6,51

138 Matthew 20,28; Mark 10,45

139 Matthew 16, 21

Notes to Chapter 6

140 Hyam Maccoby The Sacred Executioner: Human Sacrifice and the Legacy of Guilt, Thames & Hudson 1982, London

141 Mishnah Yoma 4,2; 6,2-6

142 Matthew 27, 16-25

143 Deuteronomy 21, 1-9

144 Luke 23,18-25

145 Matthew 21, 8-9, above page 131

146 2 John 1,3

147 Galatians 4,6

148 Hebrews 1,5 quoting 2 Samuel 7,14

149 Matthew 27,35

150 Mark 15,24

151 Luke 23,33-35

152 John 19, 23-24

153 Matthew 27,46. Mark 15,34

154 Geza Vermes, the Authentic Gospel of Jesus, Penguin 2003 p.194

155 Matthew 27,47

156 Or as a lion at my hands and feet

157 Singular

158 Psalm 22,11-18

159 i.e. Midrash

160 Psalm 22 (LXX 21) and the Crucifixion of Jesus- A Dissertation Presented to the Faculty of the Graduate School of Yale University, Mark George Vitalis Hoffman, 1996.

161 Plural

162 Singular

163 John 3,31 and 19,11

Notes to Chapter 7

164 Mark 5,41

165 Matthew 27, 46

166 Genesis 3,21

167 S.P. Brock, <u>Clothing Metaphors as a Means of Theological Expression in Syriac Tradition</u> in <u>Typus, Symbol, Allegorie bei den östlichen Vätern und ihren Parallelen im Mittelalter : internationales Kolloquium,</u> Eichstätt 1981.

168 Hymns of Ephrem: Hymnen de Fide ed. Beck E, Louvain 1955, pp154-5

169 Hymns of Ephrem: Carmina Nisiblena Louvain 1963, p.45

170 This translation is from the Syriac by William Wright, Apocryphal Acts of the Apostles (London, 1871), pp. 238-245. Arrangement follows A. E. J. Klijn, The Acts of Thomas (Leiden, 1962), pp. 120-125.

Notes to Chapter 8

171 Genesis 3,21

172 <u>The Fifty Spiritual Homilies and the Great Letter</u>. Trans. Maloney, George A. S. J. New York: Paulist Press, 1992 p. xi

173 Genesis 10,9

174 Pirkei d'Rabbi Eliezer 24.

175 <u>The Fifty Spiritual Homilies and the Great Letter</u>. Trans. Maloney, George A. S. J. New York: Paulist Press, 1992 p.99. The difficulty inherent in Macarius's view, and those who follow him, is that Adam names the animals before he is exiled from the Garden of Eden, whilst God does not make clothes for him until after the exile. Some have tried to resolve this by reading Genesis 3,21 as "God had made garments of skin for Adam and his wife, and clothed them". But this is not satisfactory.

176 ibid p 150

177 ibid p. 81

178 ibid p. 194

179 Matthew 9, 20-22

180 Genesis 27,15

181 Targum Pseudo Jonathan loc cit.

182 Genesis 48,22

183 The sources quoted here are quite late, possibly up to 700 years after the birth of Jesus. They are convenient as they condense and present the sequence of events quite effectively. But the ideas behind them exist, in a more scattered form in earlier sources, notably the Jerusalem Talmud, Megillah 1,11 and Syriac sources. See ‸ Louis Ginzberg, Legends of the Jews, 1913, Vol 5, p.283, n.89; S.P. Brock, 'Some Aspects of Greek Words in Syriac', in A. Dietrich (ed.), Synkretismus im syrisch-persischen Kulturgebiet (Abhandlungen der Akademie der Wissenschaften: Göttingen, 1975),pp. 98-104; 'Jewish Traditions in Syriac Sources', JJS 30 (1979), pp. 222-223.

184 For the identification of Shem with Melchizedek see chapter 11.

185 B'midbar Rabbah 4,8

186 Exodus, chapter 32

187 Exodus 32, 19

188 Numbers 3, 12

189 In Hebrew, the words for skin and light sound very similar and there is only one letter difference in the spelling.

190 Bereshit Rabbah 20,12

191 Bereshit Rabbah 84,8

192 Genesis 37,28.

193 Matthew 26,15.

194 Genesis 39,9.

195 Leviticus 8,15

196 B. Taanit 11b. The word that we have translated as unstitched can also be translated as seamless, without a border, without a hem or unembroidered. It is just as vague as the Greek word αραφοῦ which we are translating as

unstitched or seamless.

Notes to Chapter 9

197 Homer Iliad, I

198 Genesis 49,10

199 Avodah Zara 11b. The version quoted here follows the Munich Manuscript. The printed editions have "the brother of the Lord"

200 Sifrei Deuteronomy, end.

201 Leviticus chs. 13-4

202 Mishnah Yoma 6,2

203 In order to disqualify it from being offered as a sacrifice, since only unblemished animals were permitted to be sacrificed.

204 Babylonian Talmud, Gittin 55b ff.

205 Matthew 12,14

206 Matthew 23,15

207 Jots and tittles are the smallest points on a letter, or punctuation mark. The allusion here is to the well known rabbinic polemic expressed in the Talmud (Eruvin 21b and elsewhere) that the Hebrew Bible scroll is not just to be read literally. Not only the words but even each calligraphic decoration (jot and tittle) in the handwritten Torah scroll alludes to heaps upon heaps of ideas.

208 The commandments of Judaism

209 Matthew 5, 17-20

210 Epistle of Barnabas 4,11

Notes to Chapter 10

211 John 7,50

212 John 11,1 ff

213 John 12, 1-6

214 Josephus calls Mattias, son of Boethus 'one of the high priests' (Wars of the Jews 5,527) and refers to two simulta-

neous high priests, Joseph and Jeshu (ibid 6,113). This could however refer to a high priest and his deputy who would minister should the first become unfit, cf B. Yoma 47a

215 The two leading rabbis of their generation, who were converts to Judaism.

216 i.e. the converts, Shamayah and Abtalion.

217 i.e. you, the high priest

218 Talmud Yoma 71b

219 ibid 26b. The water drawing ritual took place in the autumn at the beginning of the rainy season. One of the priests performed the ritual incorrectly (it is likely that he was a Sadducee who did not consider the ritual to be valid). The congregation pelted him with the ritual fruits that they were carrying.

220 Hyam Maccoby Revolution in Judea London 1973 pp 72-3.

221 John 19,19

222 Malachi 2,7

223 Matthew 21,23

224 John 7, 14-23

225 Deuteronomy 6,9 requires all Jewish households to have a mezuzah, a parchment containing various biblical texts, on their doors.

226 Jerusalem Talmud 27d

227 Numbers 16, 8-10, italics added

228 See Babylonian Talmud Sanhedrin 43a and 106a, in the uncensored editions. These passages, as with many others which referred, or may have referred to Jesus, were ordered by Christian censors in the middle ages to be deleted.

229 Leviticus 8,23

230 Josephus Jewish War 2,118; Antiquities 18, 4-10, 23

231 Matthew 10,34-5

232 John 2, 18-20

233 Matthew 26, 61

234 Matthew 27, 50-51

235 Luke 1, 5-13

236 Luke 1, 16-17

237 The phrase "wine and strong drink" which occurs frequently in the Hebrew Bible is a catch-all for all alcoholic drinks, including beer and cider.

238 Matthew 3,4

Notes to Chapter 11

239 We don't know Paul's dates and we cannot be certain that he witnessed the destruction of the Jerusalem Temple. Nevertheless, Paul's influence carried on long after his death and we will refer to Paul and the Pauline school inter-changeably.

240 Salo W. Baron, A Social and Religious History of the Jews, vol. I (New York: Columbia University Press, 1952), pp. 170-171:

241 Galatians 2,16

242 Galatians 3,19

243 Hebrews 7, 18-19

244 Hebrews 8, 13

245 Matthew 5, 17

246 Psalm 110 1-4

247 Genesis 14, 18-20

248 Hebrews 7, 11-21

249 Hebrews 4, 14-16

250 Shem, Noah's son is equated by the Rabbis with Melchizedek. Biblical characters often have more than one name.

251 Genesis 14,18

252 Vayikra Rabbah 25,6. However, another Jewish tradition (Avot d'Rabbi Nathan 34) does identify 'my lord' in Psalm 110 with the Messiah. It is possible that Paul was aware of, and used this tradition, and that Rabbi Ishmael's exegesis was a deliberate response to this.

253 Hebrews 7,14

254 i.e. the Hebrew Bible

255 I Kings 3,1; 6,37; 7,12 and frequently.

256 Luke 24,49

257 Ireneaus attributes a Gnostic belief system to the Ebionites, which suggests that they were not just conventional Jews who believed in Jesus as a human, not a divine Messiah. But very little is known about the Ebionites, and what is known occurs only in secondary or tertiary sources. For our purposes it is enough to recognise that Judeo-Christian sects existed which continued to place Jerusalem at the centre of their practices and that consequently had a strong interest in the Jewish priesthood.

258 The difference between the theology of Paul and John was first set out systematically by George B Stevens: The Theology of Paul and of John Compared. The Biblical World, Vol. 3, No. 3 (Mar., 1894), pp. 166-175. The probability is that John remained outside the standardisation process wrought by Paul long enough to ensure that the gospel attributed to him to retained elements that had been edited out of the synoptic gospels.

Notes to Chapter 12

259 Bettenson, Henry, ed. The Early Christian Fathers: A Selection from the Writings of the Fathers from St. Clement of Rome to St. Athanasuis. Oxford: Oxford University Press, 1969. p.265

260 Alexander Roberts, D.D.& James Donaldson, Genuine Acts of Peter, from Fathers of the Third Century, Edinburgh p.263

261 Martyrdom of Polycarp, trans C.H. Hoole, 1885

262 Ad Riparium, XXII, 907

263 Josephus, Wars of the Jews Book 7, 148-151. See also Otot Hamashiach in Jellinek Bet Hamidrash II 60, Eisenstein Otzar Midrashim p. 390: "...some of the Temple treasures

that had been hidden in the palace of Julianus Caesar" and
Massechet Kelim

264 Josephus, Wars of the Jews Book 7, 148-151

BOOKS

O is a symbol of the world, of oneness and unity. In different cultures it also means the "eye," symbolizing knowledge and insight. We aim to publish books that are accessible, constructive and that challenge accepted opinion, both that of academia and the "moral majority."

Our books are available in all good English language bookstores worldwide. If you don't see the book on the shelves ask the bookstore to order it for you, quoting the ISBN number and title. Alternatively you can order online (all major online retail sites carry our titles) or contact the distributor in the relevant country, listed on the copyright page.

See our website **www.o-books.net** for a full list of over 500 titles, growing by 100 a year.

And tune in to myspiritradio.com for our book review radio show, hosted by June-Elleni Laine, where you can listen to the authors discussing their books.

MySpiritRadio